the
good
(in) the
awful

the
good
(in) the
awful

Vanessa Shepherd

ELM HILL

A Division of
HarperCollins Christian Publishing

www.elmhillbooks.com

Published in Nashville, Tennessee, by Elm Hill, an imprint of Thomas Nelson. Elm Hill and Thomas Nelson are registered trademarks of HarperCollins Christian Publishing, Inc.

Elm Hill titles may be purchased in bulk for educational, business, fund-raising, or sales promotional use. For information, please e-mail SpecialMarkets@ ThomasNelson.com.

All Scripture quotations are taken from the ESV° Bible (The Holy Bible, English Standard Version°). Copyright © 2001 by Crossway, a publishing ministry of Good News Publishers. Used by permission. All rights reserved.

Library of Congress Cataloging-in-Publication Data

Library of Congress Control Number: 2019911124

ISBN 978-1-400327461 (Paperback)
ISBN 978-1-400327478 (eBook)

For Buddy,

Your life and death were the catalysts for
teaching me some of the hardest and truest lessons.
I will cherish them always and strive to make
each one count as I hold your memory close.
And while I will forever wish that you could
have stayed a little longer, I will always be
grateful for the time that we did have together.
This is for you.

- XOXO Sissy

contents

even the
truly awful
things

And we know that

for those who love God

all things work together for good,

for those who are called

according to his purpose.

adding
value

(ROMANS 8:28)

introduction

I imagine us having coffee, you and I. Sitting around the kitchen table like old friends catching up on the newest matters of life. I imagine us laughing to the point of buckling over as we recount our journeys with the greatest sense of being fully understood and at ease. Remembering all of the ways we have made a muck of things in our own attempts (or having been caught hiding from a strong-willed three-year old who is left wondering where all of the candy went that you are most certainly eating).

And then I imagine those tears of laughter turning into the other kind of tears. The tears that tell a very different story. The story that is full of heartache and trial and pain. Where your great escape to the nearest closet has now become the spot where you now lay on its tear-stained carpet wondering how you are going to move on—or if you even can. The one where you envision yourself to be broken beyond repair with no thought as to how Humpty Dumpty will ever be put back together again. Even though you so desperately want to be put back together. Life has not afforded you that reassurance.

If I could sum this book up into one image, one signifying illustration, it would be that of a grown woman lying in the fetal position crying unrelenting tears over a loss that was so devastating and unexpected that I doubted if any good, anything of real value, could ever come from it. If this would be the thing that I would have to live with the rest of my life without any answers. Because there was no going back. It was final. And this thing, this breaking, was so "wrong" that there was no making it "right."

So on this day, the day that you and I gather around the table again, I opt to go first. I share my story. My journey through the harshest of nights filled with questions and, at times, hopelessness. And that is okay. Because I have a sneaking suspicion you know just the thing I am talking about.

Our stories may be different, but you have journeyed your

own path through the painful darkness. Do you remember it? Are you knee-deep in it right now?

This is my story but this is your story, too. The story of how we face the earth-shattering difficulties holding on to the slimmest of hopes that God is still at work. Not to restore everything to its original condition, but to build us back up using the very things that were meant to break us to begin with. The exact things that were intended and sent to destroy us. For our benefit. Our *good*. Because He sees what we cannot.

Beyond the loss (or devastation or shame or judgment or betrayal), God envisions the opportunity and the potential for another story altogether. An even greater one. One of redemption.

This is what He speaks so softly to us in Romans 8:28.

This is what Isaiah 54:17 declares over our lives.

And in all of His working and in all of His attention, He wastes nothing. No hurdle, no failure, no opposition, no devastation, and certainly no brokenness. He uses every scrap, every scar, to create something new. Not after a few years or even a few months, but right smack-dab in the middle of my mess.

That is how I want to share my story: pealing back each day, one at a time, and drawing our attention to the good thing I would have missed or wasted had it not been for a God who loves me so tenderly through and through. A God who is not afraid or ashamed of the question "What *good* can come from *this*?" but was intent instead on showing me how He would answer it.

I share my story so that you can then find the strength to share your own. Your perfectly imperfect story.

My deepest wish for you and I around this table is that we will both walk away from it more whole and healed than before. Finding our way through the darkness, together, as sojourners in a foreign land. Full of hope and dedication to the process.

It will take bravery and vulnerability, but I am up for the challenge. I've written every word with you in mind.

I will start from the beginning.

Before there was even a possibility of a breaking, when life was magical and innocent.

I will start on a happier day.

there are treasures to be found in the darkness

Saturday, May 12, 2018: My youngest sister Bethany put on the most beautiful white dress as she prepared for her big day. The ceremony was exquisite, and my husband Rich was dapper as ever as he was asked to officiate (one of the perks of having a pastor in the family).

Bethany was the youngest of four, conceived after a certain faulty "outpatient procedure," which meant a lifetime of ridicule really. She had endured all of the "oopsie baby" and "short person" jokes that a person could take as she was a notable six inches shorter than us three older siblings. Her blonde, tight curled hair, fair complexion, and freckled face contrasted our dark Middle Eastern waves and olive skin to the point that the comment "milkman's kid" had been uttered by more than just the family. It wasn't true, of course. She was fully ours. Just as ornery and witty as every last one of us.

To see her walk down the aisle and marry the man she was smitten with for more than five years was one of the highlights of my life. Despite not always being able to say so.

Seeing as we had all gathered to celebrate love and the union of the youngest of four children in our Benbow Bunch to the man who stole her heart, my brother who was still processing his own soon-to-be divorce had been attempting to get through the night the best he knew how. With a few things to help that most certainly would not gain the approval of my father.

All of the extra "help" made John a tad more friendly and outspoken than his usual pessimistic self. It was good to see him so happy as the last six months had been full of tears and moping around the house. I determined to ignore the reason he was so chipper and relented to simply enjoy his company instead.

And enjoy it I did.

Especially his impromptu speech after dinner that included a beautiful tribute to Bethany which had everyone in stitches and then in tears.

I knew that I had a long road ahead of me for the night, so I packed up before the wedding was fully over. Rich had already started ahead of me with our two boys seeing as he would be the one preaching in the morning and would need a full-ish night of sleep, but I stuck around to at least get the most important parts. The speech. The cutting of the cake. The pictures with family. And the first dance.

Everything was beautiful and exactly how Bethany had described it when she spoke of the plans Nolan (her husband) was making. I am pretty sure he was the one dreaming about it since childhood all along as she could not have cared less about anything but getting to wear cowboy boots and saying "I do." Typical last child. Along for the ride.

I hugged the newlyweds goodbye and then found myself accompanied by Stephanie (the eldest sister) and John back to my car. Harmony, Stephanie's boyfriend, had purchased a Bluetooth stereo for me as my sound system had junked out and a long road trip without music is almost as bad as a long trip talking over said tunes in my book. John decided to hook it up, which was much appreciated as my go-to tech helper was currently in a truck with my boys halfway home.

I jumped in the back seat to change out of my dress with a few tricks I learned in middle school PE that allowed for no actual skin to be shown in the process and hopped back out to say my goodbyes.

During the entire farewell, I must have received ten hugs from my very inebriated brother. It made me laugh, but I obliged every time he leaned in. He even kissed me on the cheek a few times.

Gross, I thought as I pulled away. They were just pecks but I and my bubble were ready to be in the car already. John had always been an affectionate guy, and I loved him for it; I just didn't share the same enthusiasm for personal touch.

Nonetheless, I smiled and waved as I drove away. Thinking of how much I missed them already.

- - - - - - - -

Two weeks later our family would be surrounding my brother on his hospital bed to say another kind of goodbye. Not the one where we smile and wave, saying "see you soon" as we drive away into the night, but the one where we choke back suffocating tears and beg for God to intervene with a miracle so we wouldn't have to face the darkest of days knowing what life is like without them in it.

My brother died that day. My brother *died*.

Those three words have altered the core of who I am as I have spoken them both out loud and to myself these past nine months. Sometimes as a matter of fact as describing the weather to a friend who called to chat over the phone and other times through a dense mental fog that is searching for any semblance of footing to lay hold of. It came tragically and unexpectedly, but it came nonetheless.

My brother died.

To be a great author, you have to master the art of leaving the really heartbreaking stuff for somewhere toward the end to ensure that the reader will keep turning the pages to find out what happens next, but I didn't write this story for any notoriety or accolades. I wrote it because I was hurting. I *am* hurting. And the truth is that you picked up this book on purpose, and I imagine that it is because either you have experienced some form or another of pain yourself or know someone who has. You don't need to read 100 pages into the story to find out that it hurts and it isn't fair. You are forging your way through this one simple idea that is still hard to embrace as your new reality, and it will take everything you've got. You don't need for me to wait until the most opportune time to share the crushing news of death because life didn't wait for the most opportune time.

On May 19, 2018, my brother John Paul Benbow II who was all of twenty-seven years old and full of life was involved in a freak, single-vehicle motorcycle accident. He survived one week in the Sutter Roseville Hospital Trauma Neuro ICU in Roseville, California. One week. One week of hoping and praying and crying and wrestling with the worst of myself, my faith, and this world. One week that changed every week to come after it. Everything. It changed everything.

On May 26, 2018, at 8:40 pm, my brother passed away.

There are now no small tasks. No going on "as usual," unless you take into account the new usual of sobbing through long car rides, procrastinating to get out of bed or out of the shower to give yourself just one more minute, or eating peanut butter and jelly sandwiches for dinner because cooking has now become an impossible chore. Not to mention the toll that grief and loss take on your emotional, physical, mental, and spiritual health which in turn has the power to alter every relationship you hold.

Marriage seems impossible. Friendships seem nonexistent. Families seem unbearable. And work has now become a fun game of how long I can go until oversharing and ultimately divulging a really personal fact that leaves the most uncomfortable aftertaste lingering in the room while I retreat to cover my shame. If this was a real game, I would be a winner for sure. And by winner I mean loser as I recall all of the ways I have ruined perfectly normal conversations with morbid jokes or dark facts about the end of life because I am still processing and should really let those untainted by death keep their naivety. Or at least their presumption that I am an adult and have my life together. Whatever that means anyway.

As my family and I learned of the accident and came to terms with all of the things that it could mean for John and for us, a close personal friend and woman I admire greatly sent me a message that would capture my journey better than anything I could have written myself. She simply said to "Look for God in the darkness."

My friend had been on the receiving end of many frustrated and hopeless calls when I was at my wits end throughout the past fifteen years since I had known her. She had offered comfort both when my youth pastor who held a very influential role in my life succumbed to her cancer and also when I learned that a teenage girl was infatuated with my husband leaving my marriage feeling vulnerable. She had cheered me on as I finished my bible school, as I entered into full-time ministry, and as I led a teen girl's ministry that grew from small group meetings to admittedly obnoxiously over-themed yearly conferences. She had seen the best and the worst of me over the years. She could have told me any number of things to penetrate my heart that had been, I confess, hopeless as she knew me better than most.

Instead, however, her words were those of a prayer and a challenge to do the opposite of what I could fathom doing during the worst seven days I would live thus far. The worst year really.

Look for God in the darkness.

My friend continued to expound on this idea of what it meant to go on a grand search in the middle of the night. What she said was true. "You will learn things about God and His character that you can only learn during dark seasons."

I remember this being so hard to wrap my head around, and yet rounding the corner on the first anniversary, it still holds more and more true by the day.

Last week I had the honor to attend a conference for women in ministry. One speaker stood out to me in particular as she excused her lack of deep scriptural knowledge and attaining any certificate from a traditional bible college with one breath and yet spoke with such clarity and anointing in another. I wondered why she even felt the need to confess that she had never done a master's level course on eschatological studies when she had the ability to speak directly to hearts through the power of the Holy Spirit, especially mine. She spoke to my heart that day.

I watched her pace to and fro on the center stage in front of a thousand women in the most precarious plaid suit set that only a handful of women could have pulled off (none of which being in the same age group as she spoke about her children and grandchildren in far-off countries) and heard her utter the word "grief" so intentionally over and over again. Why at women in ministry conference would grief have a place to be spoken about? I would never be able to tell you, but it was.

And it wasn't just the word that caught my attention. As she pulled out her bible to read a passage of Scripture that she jokingly prefaced with saying it was not being read "in context," my heart dropped to the floor. It read:

> I will go before you and level the exalted places, I will break in pieces the doors of bronze and cut through the bars of iron, I will give you the treasures of darkness and the hoards in secret places, that you may know that it is I, the LORD, the God of Israel, who call you by your name. For the sake of my servant Jacob, and Israel my chosen, I call you by your name, I name you, though you do not know me. I am the LORD, and there is no other, besides me there is no God; I equip you, though you do not know me, that people may know, from the rising of the sun and from the west, that there is none besides me; I am the LORD, and there is no other.
>
> (ISAIAH 45:2–6)

Maybe there isn't anything about this passage that strikes you as life changing, but as I sat there with my pink "but first coffee and then the world" notebook and a huge study bible open that

I had mistakenly grabbed instead of the one meant to be carried around that weighed significantly less, my eyes kept getting stuck on this one phrase despite everyone else finishing the passage to its completion.

"I will give you the *treasures of darkness*." Do you see it yet? *Treasures*... of *darkness*. Why these two words could be coupled together so offhandedly as if it were a natural pairing I will never understand. Because they do not seem to fit. Just as beauty for ashes, the purposes in the pain, or the gifts in the grief seemed to fight against each other. But somehow this is what God promises to "His anointed," Cyrus. Treasures of darkness. And if He promised it to him, I wondered what those treasures were for all of us.

Pain and loss are a part of life, so it is by no stretch of the imagination that you may have experienced a dark time yourself. One that left you speechless, fighting your lungs to catch its breath while you simultaneously attempted figuring out the right course of action to catch up.

I hate that hard times are inevitable. No matter how natural it is to endure struggle, it always catches you off guard. I dislike every bit of it. But what is even harder to stomach is the idea that there are "treasures" to be found in the dark places. Things that will be cherished and will hold great value for your life buried in the deepest pit of your pain.

I wish it weren't so, but after all of this time, I have come to find that the Scriptures weren't wrong. There are in fact things that I can only know about God's character or about my own self through the hardest pressing of life. It was what my friend was trying to tell me all along when she told me to "look for God in the darkness."

I have journeyed through the night when all hope was gone and all light hidden from me, and as the glimmer of a new day peaks over the horizon signaling a new sunrise and a new morning unlike any we have experienced before, I can tell you one thing: I am not walking into this new day as the same girl. The light is still yet to fully break through the clouds that remain from the storms, but there is just enough shining through the cracks to see the treasures I now carry. The things that I have knowingly and unknowingly picked up as I journeyed through.

Each item is something that I now celebrate, and it is my sincerest hope to share them with you so that you too can face the darkest nights or harshest realities of mornings when the finality of your situation sets in confirming that things will never be the same again, with hope and strength and faith. I wish that it were easy and that each lesson could be bought as a gift, showing up to your door in two to three business days, but these truths, while worth the world, cannot be purchased. They have to be fought for. A piece of yourself has to die in order to receive them. If only there were any other way I would tell you so, but this is the only way.

My friend, I know the pain. Not the way you know it because every story is its own. Everything that is lost is unique to both the one who loses it and the thing that is lost. I am not urging you to compare your story with mine to determine which is better or worse. What I am praying for is that you accept my invitation to look for God in your own stormy passage through the night seasons. To rip up every rock and hard place until the thing that has escaped you becomes as strong and secure as your foundation.

Like the man who found himself in a field that was unfamiliar to him in Matthew 13. A land that he had never been in before. And yet Jesus says to him: "The kingdom of heaven is like treasure hidden in a field, which a man found and covered up. Then in his joy he goes and sells all that he has and buys that field" (Matthew 13:44). This is exactly what it is like to see more of Heaven in our lives. It means venturing into unknown waters and stumbling upon something that we will spend our whole lives on. It means discovering beauty in tragedy and holding on to it with great joy despite knowing that it costs us everything.

This world will take enough of our lives as it is. I am in it to see the redemption. The good thing that God promises to work my situation into despite it not being there yet. I need Him to work it for not just my benefit but for the benefit of anyone who may find himself watching. So I can both hold the treasure closely like this man in Scripture and also as high up as I can reach declaring it for the many that go before or after who need to know where the treasure is. To know that there *is* treasure to be found.

I want to look into the puny face of the enemy of our souls and see him squirm when I hold it out and declare that everything he took from me, from my family, and from our futures here on this earth is nothing in comparison to what I will take from him with and through the power of God. Because I will not stop.

I won't stop looking for the purposes of God in the tough places and inviting others to join in the journey so that one day, they too can enter into the kingdom of Heaven—all the while I declare over each one that "this is for my brother." Because it is.

For my brother and for yours. For the job you lost or the marriage that crumpled. For the grandmother that met her Maker or the child that never had the opportunity to enter this world. For the friend who chose to leave or the sibling addicted to drugs. We are doing it for them and for us so that God can show Himself as exactly who He proclaimed Himself to be—the Redeemer of all things.

The darkness will be a part of all of our stories, but I know that there are treasures to be found. I know it because I have found some already. And for the rest of my life, I have committed myself to finding them. Lessons that I have learned because I chose the hard task of looking for Him when all hope seemed lost, and everyone else had already jumped ship. It wasn't pretty. In fact it looked a lot like fumbling around on my hands and knees with an outstretched hand to find something that would offer any kind of safety or protection from the onslaught of attacks and bad news, through tears and pleading with Him to come to our rescue. But I found them.

This journey isn't perfect and it won't make you feel good, but I have a deep-in-my-gut feeling that it is just what you need. So find your shovel and your work clothes, and join me in the great unknown. Because we are going on a treasure hunt—and it is going to get messy.

Whenever God said anything, it happened, which means that I can trust that God will do just this - cause light to come from our dark places

For God, who said, 'Let light shine out of darkness,' has shone in our hearts to give the light of the knowledge of the glory of God in the face of Jesus Christ. But we have this treasure in jars of clay, to show that the surpassing power belongs to God and not to us. We are afflicted in every way, but not crushed; perplexed, but not driven to despair; persecuted, but not forsaken; struck down, but not destroyed; always carrying in the body the death of Jesus, so that the life of Jesus may also be manifested in our bodies.

(2 CORINTHIANS 4:6-10)

if you are
hurting,
God is close

Saturday, May 19, 2018: The text that started it all came through on my silenced phone. My husband who had been grouped in on the message with me read it first and then peaked over the coffee table from his place on the ground to ask if I too had read the text from my dad. I hadn't.

I shifted around to find where my phone had fallen, and during the middle of a perfectly beautiful weekend spent watching movies with my family and entertaining guests, my world changed.

I sat there for a moment. Elbows on my knees trying to process my father's words.

"Don't tell your mother yet but your brother has been in an accident and your sister is on the way to the hospital," it read.

John Paul had been in a motorcycle mishap a few years prior, but there was no such text to warn us immediately after. Just the slightly jaded yet hilariously rehearsed version of what happened at the next family night told by my brother himself who walked away with an injured finger. I can still see him visibly flustered that his middle finger could not work independent of another finger as they were now splinted together. For some reason John found great amusement in that one finger and used it often. This time, however, it was much different.

When my initial shock had worn off, I rose from my seat and walked into my bedroom to give my older sister a call to find out more about the situation as she was sure to be the first on site.

"Hello?"

Her voice sounded laser-focused. That is how Stephanie has always been, good in emergency situations. She was the eldest of four, and taking charge, especially in chaos, was her specialty.

Truly, her ability to emotionally detach in the middle of crisis was a gift. I, on the other hand, go numb. My brain does not function at hyper-speed, but does the opposite—it hibernates.

I am so glad that it was her that they had called as she was both the closest in distance from the hospital and the best person to process what she was about to walk into. For better and for worse.

She placed me on speaker phone as she was still driving and I forced out the words, "Dad sent me a text, Steph. What happened?"

"The hospital called me. John was in a motorcycle accident. They wouldn't tell me anything else over the phone but they said that I needed to get here right away."

I tried to focus in on what she was saying, but I really only cared about one detail... "But he's alive?" I could feel my throat close and water fill my eyes as I was putting all of the pieces together.

"Yes, Sis. He's alive."

What followed next was an overwhelming amount of tears that wouldn't stop from flowing as my body allowed me to process more and more of what was happening with my not-so-baby baby brother. Followed shortly by the worst anxiety of my life and desperate urge to be by his side.

She was pulling up to the hospital, so I let her get off of the phone, pleading with her to give me an update as soon as she had it.

Time has never crept forward so slowly. I had an eerie feeling that this time was much different than before and started frantically throwing laundry into a bag. I didn't even check to see if each item was clean or not. And then the phone rang again. It was Stephanie. My hands were shaking so bad that it took way too much effort to accept the call on my "smart device."

"Hi Steph. Did you see John?"

"Yes. I saw him. I talked to him."

"Oh, good. So he is still awake," I think this is where I first let the air that I was holding hostage in my lungs go.

"Yes. He never lost consciousness."

"Oh, I am so glad to hear that. How is he? What are they saying?"

Her tone changed. "Ahnna," a nickname Steph has had for me

all of my life, one I have come to cherish deeply, until this moment when it felt like I didn't want to hear it... "He can't move anything from the chest down. It could be temporary nerve damage but right now he's paralyzed."

Paralyzed. When you hear that word, when you read that word, do you feel the heaviness that comes with it, too? Do you switch from involuntarily taking breaths to forcing yourself to breathe in and out because you just forgot how? Because I do. Even still, now, I do.

Those tears that I thought were too many to number before were nothing in comparison to this new wave of heartbreak that I was experiencing.

All that I could get out was, "but he's alive, right?". As if somehow this devastating news had changed his predicament in the last few minutes. Because life-altering tragedy was enough, we could figure that out as a family, but I could not do the loss of his life. I just couldn't.

I think she understood what I was saying as I most assuredly think she felt it too. "Yes, Sis. He's alive."

We said our goodbyes, and I waited for my parents to come pick me up as dad had finally shared with my mother what was going on. With Stephanie able to confirm the brevity of his situation, they were planning their trip up north, picking me up on their way.

What followed next was an excruciating five-hour drive from the Central Coast to the place they had just moved from two days prior. *We'll unpack that later* (pun intended).

Five hours of crying and talking and listening to someone who likes to process bad news while chomping on the loudest most potent-smelling food. That wasn't me. No, I was the one in the back seat of the truck with my nose pressed against the window praying for a gust of wind to break through the glass and into my nostril because I never wanted to eat again.

Just a few minutes into our road trip, my father had turned up the Christian radio to fill the void of silence that we had filled with mounting questions and the whole gamut of human emotions, and the oddest thing happened. The radio host was talking about faith and hope. Now of course that doesn't sound very odd as we had the stereo tuned to a Christian station, but the way she talked about holding onto faith was like God Himself was sitting in the truck and speaking to us.

My dad broke the silence that had washed over the start of our journey as we listened to her words by saying, "this is for us." And I knew it was, too. There was no point in imagining all levels of horror just yet, as nothing was for certain. What we needed to do was be silent and to listen and to hold onto faith.

- - - - - - - -

In the weeks that would follow, there were many times that I would be tempted to kick into fifth gear and go full speed into the "what ifs." What if my parents had never moved? What if John had never purchased a motorcycle? What if he and his wife had never separated? What if, what if, what if???

In all of my frustrations and anxieties, I would feel more and more distant from a loving God. A God who promises to "never leave [us] or forsake [us]" (Hebrews 13:5). A God described as both a Good Shepherd who cares for His sheep and a Father who looks after His children. Where was He in all of this? Where was the good in all of this? Because it was feeling more and more like I was on my own and needed one of those self-help books that tell me to find the strength within myself which was really all nonsense being as there was no strength to be found.

On one terribly lonely day, I remember asking God where He had hid Himself. Because that is exactly what it felt like. Like He was hiding. And He answered in a way that I did not expect. *Through my own voice.*

The week after John's funeral, I had started back to work. My parents were still attempting to unpack the home that they had just rented in Grover Beach to be close to my husband and I in an effort to help the church after my dad's retirement. I committed to coming over most nights to help them unpack. One evening while driving home from their house to ours, I found myself in the car with our two boys along the coastline late into the night. I, as I often do, pointed to the vast expanse of water and instructed them to "look at the ocean"! I wanted them to look at it as often as possible to both be grateful for the incredible place that God has allowed us to live and pastor and be reminded of how big our God really is despite my own struggles with seeing Him at work in my life as of late.

It always gets a lot of squeals and screeches of excitement as we all have a general fondness for the water. Except this time... this time it was the middle of the night, and there was no telling the end of the ocean from the beginning of the sky.

Everything was dark.

In that moment Jacob, who was six years old and enjoys understanding all manners of life by questioning things until either he comprehends the answer, or I give up, astutely stated, "I don't see it." To which I smiled and reassured him, "well it's there" (knowing that I may have just gotten myself into a pickle should he be in the mood to question further). To my surprise, that curious little almost-first grader only had one response.

He simply asked, "Are you sure?"

It seemed elementary enough as I chuckled out an "I'm sure" as if something really might have the power to move an entire ocean, and then I startled myself as God began to show me my own unbelief. I was the child in the back seat peering out into a world of darkness asking if the very thing we have always counted on, I have always counted on, somehow moved without my knowing.

The sea has always been one of the biggest reminders of God's presence in my life as He merely spoke it into existence. Its beauty would often remind me of His good plans for us, and I would rest in the tossing to and fro of my body small in comparison to its greatness as it would wash over whatever small anxieties I might be facing at the time. I knew God was still in control despite my attempts at navigating a small boogie board over its waves or wading through its waters atop a kayak. Don't even get me started on surfing, I will never even attempt that again.

It's funny though, isn't it? How assured we are when things are going just right that God's presence is all around us and yet as soon as trouble arises, it is the first thing we question?

Where are you, God?

That is what we say, as if our situation had the power to move Him. I was wrong. The darkness may have covered His existence for a while, but it could not cause Him to not exist.

He is as gentle as a soft word of faith coming through the radio and as steady as my father's hunger in emergency situations. Ok that last one was just for kicks and giggles and maybe because I am still a little traumatized by his constant need for food. But you get the point.

My dad has always been one of the hardest workers I have ever known, at one point working three jobs to support our family of six. This of course meant that he would be gone for longer periods at a time which also meant missing out on seeing us receive awards or going to concerts together or being around for silly crying sessions when Bobby from school gave me flowers and embarrassed the snot out of me. Mom was there, though. She handled it like a boss.

In one particularly hard season of life, aka junior high, I decided to try my hand at cross country. I remember the last meet and making my only goal to "not be the last one to finish," which looked like it was going to happen as I started down the last stretch toward the finish line. My body was tired, I didn't have anything left in me, and then I heard a sound that would crush my dreams. Footsteps. Hard and fast footsteps that sounded as if they were right behind me as the girl in last place was about to pass by.

I felt so defeated. I wanted to stop right there. I wanted to throw in the towel and walk away, crying as I went. And just as I felt at my lowest another familiar sound filled the air.

"You can do it Vanessa!"

It was my father's voice.

He was working in the area and snuck away to see my last meet. And while he could have been so disappointed and stayed silent not to alert anyone that he was present or that I was his, he decided instead to cheer me on. In his cheering, he claimed me, even though I finished last.

"But you finished," he said as he embraced my weary body.

This is the image I get of God whenever I imagine myself at my lowest. When the Scriptures say that God is "near to the broken-hearted and saves the crushed in spirit" (Psalm 34:18). I imagine a God that rushes in. I hear Him calling out our name and cheering us on to finish the race. The whole passage is even more beautiful when read in context as David writes:

> When the righteous cry for help, the LORD hears and delivers them out of all their troubles. The LORD is near to the brokenhearted and saves the crushed in spirit. Many are the afflictions of the righteous, but the LORD delivers him out of them all.
>
> (PSALM 34:17–19)

When a child lets out a cry for help, do you imagine that a good father idly sits by until they get their life together? Or until they sooth their own pain? Of course not. A good father rushes in at even the hint of a broken heart to comfort and soothe their child even if it means that they are still hurting while he is present. Sometimes a parent can't fix it right away. Sometimes cleaning it out and placing a Band-Aid on it is all that they can do. But the Band-Aid isn't what makes the child better—it's the sight their mother or father rushing in.

This is what our Good Father does. There are many times in Scripture where He instructs us to "draw near to Me and I will draw near to You" or "seek Me and you will find Me when you search for Me with all of your heart" which implies that we make the first action. We are the ones to move. But nowhere does it say that when you are hurting, you have to be the one to move. When you are broken, you have to find a way to hobble to the Lord. No, God is the one who comes running. In fact Scriptures even say that "He heals the brokenhearted and binds up their wounds" (Psalm 147:3).

The situation may not change right then and there. The outcome may not be miraculously altered. You may just have a bandage or a stint from where He bound you up, and you will most definitely have that scar the rest of your life. But when you were hurting, when you were desperate, and when you were on the brink of giving up, you can be sure that God was there.

That was one of the first lessons of truth that He gifted me in the dark place. Despite my wallowing and tantruming at how things were going, He softly reminded me that He was there for the whole thing. And that He wanted me to stop hysterically screaming for a brief moment so that I could realize it.

Maybe it is just my children, but in the middle of a fit, it appears that my kids have the potential to lose all control of their feelings, truth, and their surroundings. They just lose it. Also, sometimes I join in and become a big baby. It is exhausting as the mother. But if my boys can do a few simple things in the process of their struggling with pain, it opens the door for my being able to comfort them.

I only wonder how much more the Lord could comfort us if we were to do the same.

The first is the easiest and the hardest. I imagine God speaking to me how I do with our boys in the middle of their hysterics.

Just stop. Quiet yourself. And be still.

If we don't stop what we are doing when we are in the middle of an emotional downhill spiral, then we will never be able to discern what is going on around us because we will be too busy pitching a fit. Nor will we be able to allow anything or anyone to come close enough to comfort us. Even when the pain is unbearable.

If it seems impossible because what you are facing is too great, just remember the words of Psalm 46.

God is our refuge and strength, a very present help in trouble. Therefore we will not fear though the earth gives way, though the mountains be moved into the heart of the sea, though its waters roar and foam, though the mountains tremble at its swelling. *Selah*

There is a river whose streams make glad the city of God, the holy habitation of the Most High. God is in the midst of her; she shall not be moved; God will help her when morning dawns. The nations rage, the kingdoms totter; he utters his voice, the earth melts.

The LORD of hosts is with us; the God of Jacob is our fortress. *Selah*

Come, behold the works of the LORD, how he has brought desolations on the earth. He makes wars cease to the end of the earth; he breaks the bow and shatters the spear; he burns the chariots with fire.

Be still, and know that I am God. I will be exalted among the nations, I will be exalted in the earth!

The LORD of hosts is with us; the God of Jacob is our fortress. *Selah*

Of course, it takes more than quieting ourselves to really settle down. The strangest thing happens when my boys are in moments of excruciatingly painful situations. When I have finally gotten them to stop flailing their arms or screaming directly into my eardrum, I look down at their faces and realize that these kids have forgotten how to breathe.

I get it. It's hard. I know. It sucks. But do you know what is worse? Passing out because you deprived your brain of oxygen. And with spiritual things, it is the same. If you forget the Scriptures, which is the Word of God, the very breath of life—you will perish also. So what God breathed out, take a minute to breathe in!

> You, however, have followed my teaching, my conduct, my aim in life, my faith, my patience, my love, my steadfastness, my persecutions and sufferings that happened to me at Antioch, at Iconium, and at Lystra—which persecutions I endured; yet from them all the Lord rescued me. Indeed, all who desire to live a godly life in Christ Jesus will be persecuted, while evil people and impostors will go on from bad to worse, deceiving and being deceived. But as for you, continue in what you have learned and have firmly believed, knowing from whom you learned it and how from childhood you have been acquainted with the sacred writings, which are able to make you wise for salvation through faith in Christ Jesus. All Scripture is breathed out by God and profitable for teaching, for reproof, for correction, and for training in righteousness, that the man of God may be complete, equipped for every good work.
>
> (2 TIMOTHY 3:10–17)

His Words are life to our weary bones, but we will never hear them if we aren't also taking a moment to listen.

Have you ever heard or thought, "It's going to fall off isn't it," after you crushed your hand in the door for the four-thousandth time? Because I have. It didn't make it true or even close to reality, but we think the strangest, most obtuse things when we are feeling pain. And this, this is why it is so important to listen when we are hurting. Because oftentimes our emotions are spinning all kinds of stories that have nothing to do with truth or faith, and we can so easily get caught up in them. (I hope you caught that spider web visual because it is exactly what I think of when I think of the lies we believe.)

If you make the hard but right choice to stop yourself and breathe in the Word of God, then make sure you also take a moment to pause and listen for His voice. Because it will be speaking truth. Like a parent consoling their injured child, whispering all of the things they are certain of. Like the finger not needing to be amputated or the hand not falling off. God is speaking to us in our pain. Through a friend. Through your pastor. Through the Holy Spirit. Or through the radio. Just listen.

> My sheep hear my voice, and I know them, and they follow me. I give them eternal life, and they will never perish, and no one will snatch them out of my hand. My Father, who has given them to me, is greater than all, and no one is able to snatch them out of the Father's hand. I and the Father are one.
>
> (JOHN 10:27–30)

As much as I would love to say that being still, breathing, and listening will change our situations, the truth is that sometimes it won't. Most of the time even. But it will change *us*.

And it doesn't make it fair or right or good, but that doesn't negate that it is still the truth. That there are some situations that won't change. The miracle will never come. The prayer will not be answered the way we prayed for it to be. That was the reality we had to face. And while I believe our story to still be the best example of God's relentless love to us in our lives (which you will just have to read further to understand how I can even make that statement), it also includes a lot of pain that was final.

I will never again see here on this earth my brother hobbling down the hall with his arms above his head like a chimpanzee telling me to give him a hug. I will never hear him screech out "Sissy" in the way that only he could, higher than any one of us three sisters could speak. I will never again be able to read the texts about his newest promotion or his sarcastic recounting of how amazing he is at whatever he puts his hand to despite having zero credentials or degrees. And I am not jumping at the chance to accept this, but I still have to accept it.

And as much as I have to allow this reality to sink in, I also have to accept the love and comfort of a Father who knows that I am hurting, knows that life is full of moments of loss, and knows that everything here is broken. He knows. That is the whole point of Him sending His Son. Because this world is hurting and lost and broken. He is not debating that with you. What He is saying instead is, let Me be close to you. Let Me come near you so that I can bind up your wounds. Let Me hold you and whisper the truth of redemption into your ears. Not to justify anything, but to remind you that He won't let it go to waste. Not even your pain. Especially your pain.

It is why I am so certain that if you are hurting, God is close by. As familiar as the voice on the radio or a father pointing out what we may have missed in our worrying. Those words of hope and faith, that was for us.

my part:
holding fast.
trusting God.
praying.

Because he (holds) fast to me in love, I <u>will</u> deliver him; I

<u>will</u> protect him, because he knows my name. When he

calls to me, I <u>will</u> answer him; I <u>will</u> be with him in

trouble; I <u>will</u> rescue him and honor him. With long life

I <u>will</u> satisfy him and show him my salvation.

(PSALM 91:14-16)

Pro Tip: Replace the he and him in this
verse with your name and read it as God's
promise to you! Write it down and post it
around your house to remind your soul that
God is with you in this. He hasn't left!

all pain
is painful

Sunday, May 20, 2018: My parents and I had pulled up to the hospital the night before and wasted no time rushing in to see John after the doctors had finished being with him to run their latest test, namely, CTs, blood draws, and scans of his lungs, whatever they could do at the moment they thought of it. We trickled in two at a time of course as he was stationed in an ICU room with round-the-clock nurse attention and limited room for guests.

Stephanie and I peeked into the room after my parent's visit, and there laid my baby brother. A swollen bruised and scabbed face, tube jammed down his throat to help his lungs breathe… and hair, the most magnificent head of hair I have ever seen. I kid you not.

John Paul lifted his hands ever so slightly signaling his wanting a hug which I gladly reciprocated. I knew his injuries were extensive, so I held back as much of my weight as possible shifting to my heels as I leaned in. It was both a mixture of relief and utter devastation to see him, but I did not let it crumble me. I just stood by his bedside as he motioned for the pad of paper he had been using to scribble on to communicate and read as he told me "I am paralyzed" and "take a picture of my face" so he could see what he looked like. I did. It was the prettiest pavement mauled face I had ever seen. But all John could see, past his swollen eye with already terrible vision, was the missing teeth that had been knocked out in the impact and the fact that he was lying in a bed that he would never be able again to pull himself up from.

I don't know if you have ever stood beside as someone realized their own devastation, but it is the most helpless feeling I have ever experienced in my entire life.

I wanted to cry with him. I wanted to tell him how sorry I was. I wanted to blame someone, something, for his situation. But that isn't in us. The Benbows are notorious for using humor to cope with our pain and sarcasm to tackle hard topics. So that is what we did. We smiled and attempted a laugh. And then I watched as he ran his finger up and down his abdomen, trying to learn the extent of his paralysis and if any feeling had been regained.

It hadn't.

His finger hovered just above his nipple, moving it ever so slightly in every direction with small hopes, but upon examining the desolation on his face, he knew what we all knew. It was still too early to tell, but it seemed he would be a paraplegic the remainder of his life. I looked up at Stephanie who had been with him for most of the day and studied her face. Sad but steady. I prayed for an ounce of the steadiness she had.

By the time the clock had struck midnight, my youngest sister, her new husband, and even John's wife had arrived to join my sister, parents, cousin, and I as we all took turns spending time by John's bedside to keep him company. He was mostly in a medicated slumber so as not to pull out his intubation tube, which he completely despised, but none of the tribe that had accumulated in the hospital waiting room, waiting for their turn, had found one comfortable position to sleep in for more than an hour or so. This made each and every one of us *bona fide* zombies come the morning. Genuinely, I do not know that any of us had slept at all.

As the early light of morning drew on, doctors began to share more and more news. It wasn't looking great, truth be told. One even stated that they had struggled to figure out what to do at all as they had never seen someone in John's condition survive the initial impact of the accident. They rattled off injury after injury that my brother had sustained on that winding road in the foothills of Auburn:

A fracture to his C2 vertebrae
Fractures to ribs 3–8
Fractured T3–T7 vertebrae
Severed and displaced spinal cord

Tension hemopneumothorax (punctured right lung)
Traumatic brain injury
Epidural hematoma
Basilar skull fracture
Orbital fracture
A maxillary sinus fracture
A fracture to his right clavicle bone
Five arterial bleeds

A doctor who looked no older than eighteen years old came in to share that John was scheduled for a back reconstructive surgery to adjust his obliterated spine into something that resembled a more natural curvature later that morning to give him the best chance at sitting upright in a chair. There was no timeframe on how long it would take, just that he needed it done and we would be there when it was over.

The scene inside of that waiting room looked much different during the daylight. Family members waiting for their own loved ones to get out of surgery started to pour in where our family had once taken up every available square inch by sprawling out our tired legs onto the accompanying chairs or resting our heads under arm rests,. We all anxiously awaited for signs of "our" doctor to walk through the door, keeping our eyes constantly shifting between the hall and the monitor on the wall that listed surgery numbers and status. We had no idea which number was John's. Just of the plethora that were not.

Finally in the late afternoon after eight grueling hours, Doogie Howser (a reference for my older friends who remember the television show about a child prodigy-turned-doctor) came in to update us. He popped up onto the counter that spanned the entirety of the one wall and began to share some equally heartbreaking yet hopeful news.

He was undoubtedly and unchangeably *paralyzed*.

His spinal cord, while in the general area for where it needed to be, was still severed beyond repair. And while it was the worst injury the doctor had ever seen, John's sats stayed stable for the entire surgery allowing him to be fitted in the near future for a back brace to help his spine continue to heal without further complications. One year he would have to wear it while he stayed in a program close to the hospital that would serve as a rehab to teach him how to function again independently. One year. And then after that year, we would reassess, and he might even be able to live on his own as he was healthy and young and there were so many facilities that catered to people with disabilities, specifically those confined to a wheelchair.

The thought of my brother now being known to society as disabled made me sick to my stomach, but I tried to focus on how thankful I was that he survived. That he was still with us. Because he very well shouldn't have been.

- - - - - - - -

I have spent many days in a waiting room, not just during this terribly awful ordeal, but especially during 2015 (the year we deemed should not be named) when our family endured one trial after another.

My mother was diagnosed with stage 4 colorectal cancer and underwent an extreme surgery and chemotherapy.

My father broke his back three times causing pieces of his spine to lodge in his sciatic nerve which resulted in debilitating pain.

My brother developed the deadly C. diff infection after being sent home with antibiotics for other infections not once but twice from the hospital.

My older sister's insides literally exploded (ok well maybe just the giant cysts that were forming on her ovaries) causing her to be minutes from bleeding out.

And then there was the awkward growing concern with my body freaking out on me as I would wake up each day with less and less sensation… everywhere.

Waiting rooms are not where you want to spend the majority of your day when your left leg is numb and you can no longer feel whatever items you are holding in your hands. Especially if they are your own children. Waiting rooms also mean sitting in a crowded room full of sick people as you wait for your appointment time with all of the hacks and coughs that come with it. Even if you aren't sick, nine times out of ten you will be by the time you leave.

When I had been in and out of doctors' offices to run all kinds of tests that one frustrating year, the one we thought would be the worst, I jokingly came up with four stages of waiting similar to the five stages of grief. I thought it was so funny until I realized how accurate the list was. It went something like this:

Stage 1: Anticipation

Everyone is filled with anticipation upon first arriving to any appointment and taking their seat in the waiting room. It is the most exciting out of all of the stages. Full of hope and trust in God because we know our Bibles and Psalm 37:4 promises us that if we "delight [ourselves] also in the Lord" that "He will give [us] the desires and secret petitions of [our] hearts." Doesn't that sound incredible?

This is the stage where rainbows and butterflies exist and your name is going to be the one they call next. The one where dreams are possible, answers are guaranteed, and waiting won't last forever. This stage, I have a love–hate relationship with this stage. It's hopeful and beautiful and, more times than not, a giant bowl full of crap. Have you heard the verse about "hope deferred [making] the heart sick" (Proverbs 13:12)? Well I am pretty sure it was written for just such a stage as this.

Once anticipation wears off, we get hit like a ton of bricks by stage number two.

Stage 2: Anxiety

The questions start coming in like a flood. Did you miss your name being called? Are you in the right office, on the right day? What if you don't get the answers you were hoping for? The questions have a way of taking over; they have the ability to silence absolutely everything else in your life and paralyze you from the head down. They are all consuming and all controlling. And as beautiful as the sentiment is to "be anxious for nothing, but in everything by prayer and supplication, with thanksgiving, let your requests be made known to God" (Philippians 4:6), it is way easier said than done.

Anxious thoughts have a way of being put down and then picked back up time and time again.

Can we truly pray about such things and be free instantly from our anxiety? Or is it best understood as a continual prayer to keep our hearts focused on the right things? Whatever the case, anxiety soon leads to something I have a feeling all of us have experienced at least once not just in our lifetime, but sometimes daily.

Stage 3: Anger

Your once harmless thoughts have now turned to something far greater. You start to look around and get angered at how many are being called in before you. How many have received their answers and seen the doctors, who have barely just arrived.

Hello? You were totally here well before them? Why can't they go in order? Is it something you did or didn't do?

You shoot glares across the room to the patients, to the nurses, and to anyone who is not making what you came in for a priority. It's not personal but it feels personal.

Anger has a way of creeping in every time we decide to compare our lives with the lives of others. Our timelines with theirs. But who are we truly mad at? Them for coming to the doctor's office or the doctor for seeing them first? I have a sneaking suspicion that many of us have some misplaced anger with God that we are taking out on people, because He is doing for them what we have been asking Him to do for us.

Just a few short verses after reading how God would give us the desires of our heart, David instructs us to "rest in the Lord, and wait patiently for Him; Do not fret because of him who prospers in his way... cease from anger, and forsake wrath; do not fret—it only causes harm." (Psalm 37:7–8). It wasn't unintentional for David to link the two—our waiting for answers and getting angry with others who have gotten theirs—because it happens, every time.

But when we allow ourselves to go through each of these stages keeping God's word in mind, it always leaves us with this last thing.

Stage 4: Acceptance

I know we talked about acceptance in a different form in the last chapter, but when we accept the waiting seasons or the painful seasons where we are being healed but not healed yet, there is far more at stake. More than just us or our own lives.

It is only in this stage that we find ourselves committed to the waiting, understanding that it is necessary and that our being there is completely unrelated to everything and everyone else. We stop obsessing about the answers and start to look around. We examine the posters on the walls, the childish choice of movies playing, and the people that we were once infuriated by become more human. It was in this stage that God spoke to my heart so clearly when I had been in the waiting room for some time after the fourth or fifth test had been run—something that He could have only said when I was still, committed, and at peace.

I had been in this one waiting room for almost an hour; the place had emptied itself twice, and my name had yet to be called. At first there was anticipation, then anxiety, and then anger, but I had finally made my way into acceptance. I found myself watching *Brave* on the small TV tucked in the corner across the room when there was some small commotion behind me. I turned around to find a woman who had dropped something and a man, a stranger to her, jumping in to help her pick it up. She smiled, thanked him, and took her seat. Honestly, it was beautiful.

And then there was a woman there with her mother. I watched as they laughed and talked with such passion for life. They were unfazed by how long they had been there or how many had gone before them because they were there together, and being together was enough. Enough to silence the unanswered questions or the problems they were facing. Their love for each other was evident, and their waiting full of joy. It too was beautiful.

But my attention was quickly stolen by the sound of a mother trying to soothe her crying baby. She paced, she talked, she sang, and she tried everything without any relief from that little girl's shrieks of discontentment. I have been there before. I didn't even want to venture out of the house when our youngest was two and three years old. It's miserable and embarrassing, and I couldn't help but feel pity for her.

Just as soon as I had realized all that was going on around me, my name was called and I heard it loudly. Not my name, although it had been called and caused me to rise from my chair and move toward the nurse motioning to take me back, but I heard Him speak so softly to my heart, "don't waste the wait."

I knew what He meant. I knew exactly what He was telling me.

I had spent over an hour so focused on myself and my

problems and my questions that I forgot to lift my eyes to see the world around me. Not the newest update on politics or where our world is headed, not the opinions shouted loudly in the most inappropriate of places, but the people I had been placed with in the waiting room.

I was so caught up in me that I forgot about everyone else. I was selfish. And instead of condemnation, I felt the conviction of God rise up on the inside of me. Not a hateful *"you wasted it,"* but a challenge for the many waiting rooms I would continue to find myself in—"don't waste the wait," He said.

That moment has always stuck with me, and now just a few short years later, I was finding myself in a similar situation being faced with a similar choice. Would our pain be so crippling and all-consuming that it would wash out the pain of anyone else who entered? While we were sitting and pacing and praying and talking with each other, we saw family after family come in to wait for their own news. Good news and bad news, all kinds of news. We had no idea how long John's surgery would take, but we passed the time by keeping our eyes open to really seeing people.

I love this about my family. It was ingrained in us from childhood when my father would buy an extra meal for a homeless person sitting near the drive thru or my mother who would hear about a need in someone's life that they would secretly meet, to have compassion and care for others. No matter our own situation. Sometimes especially in spite of our own situation. And waiting for news of my brother would be no different.

Two other families waited while their husbands/sons were brought in after being in a motorcycle accident. I watched them worry and toil and wring their hands as I had been doing all morning.

One family gathered for a grandparent in surgery after a fall.

Despite their advanced age, this person was still the pillar of the family leaving many distraught and in fear for what may be.

And then there was this beautiful family whose son was admitted that day after his sister brought him in barely responsive. Everyone else had received their good news and carried on for the day, but this one family would make the journey with us. The one where the hospital waiting room would now become our homes, the constant rotation of nurses and doctors all with their own ideas of what may help were no comfort, and the lifeless saunter up and down the halls would offer no relief.

These were our fellow sojourners. The sisters pleading for their brother's life. The father begging God for a miracle. The mother attempting to hold it all together as her child, her only son, lay in a bed with every Hail Mary imaginable being thrown.

If we had been so focused on our own plight, we would have missed it. We would have missed them. They didn't know our John or our pain, but they knew pain. They knew what it felt like because they were feeling it too. And that is the whole point. Not everyone will go through your experiences of pain and grief, but everyone will experience pain and grief.

This does not diminish your story. But it also shouldn't diminish others' as well. We have to validate that others can be hurting when we are hurting, too. The world doesn't take turns. And sometimes hurting people will hurt people, and there is no exemption for that during the really hard stuff.

I am choosing to let this mold me into a better, more compassionate person. The kind that finds the others discarded to the pit when I am there myself. Not to form our own little sad group to rebel against God as if our suffering were some kind of proof that He isn't good, but to fulfill the law of Christ by sharing in the burden. Even if it means my brother's death being compared to the pain someone felt when they lost their pet. I kid you not. I almost lost my mind. But looking back, that was painful for them, and I am glad that I didn't make it more painful by doing something I would have regretted. God knows I wanted to.

Our names were not called first that Sunday in the waiting room. In fact we were one of the last names called that day. But what the Lord did in that room was more than put us in some dark and twisted holding pattern taunting us with the worst what ifs a person could wrestle with. No, He gave us an unexpected community.

A reason to step back from the accident that had sucked us in to realize that there were others hurting in the world around us. Among us even. And instead of that making us feel worse or even overwhelmed, there was an odd peace and familiarity that filled the room. We rooted for good reports for their son, and they cried with us when John would pass first knowing that their son would shortly follow.

When I think of that week, I think how God must have known exactly what we were going through as He too had to watch His only Son be crucified and pass from the earth, far from His presence. Pain is not unknown to Him. This is why we can run to Him and cry "Abba Father" because He understands our plight. He doesn't say that it has to measure up to some fictional level of suffering in order for Him to be concerned.

There is no scale for pain.

I hope you really processed that. Because it is what allows us to remain tender hearted instead of becoming stone cold when we face adversity. It is the reason that we can look on others with compassion instead of anger when their dog dying is the same to them as the loss of a human life. Or their boyfriend breaking up with them institutes an emergency counseling session as you grapple with the mortal exit of your only brother. *There is no scale of pain.*

All pain is painful.

And because Jesus walked this earth and faced the things that we are still facing today, He can understand more than anyone what

ALL PAIN IS PAINFUL

it feels like to be wounded. So join me in opening that metaphorical bedroom door like a toddler who knows just how much they belong there as a child and heir to tell our Good Father just exactly where it hurts. Because it does. Still. No matter the reason why or the reasons you think it still shouldn't, He is waiting.

For we do not have a high priest who is unable to

sympathize with our weaknesses, but one who in every

respect has been tempted as we are, yet without sin. Let

us then with confidence draw near to the throne of

grace, that we may receive mercy and find grace to help

in time of need.

(HEBREWS 4:15-16)

*He gives grace because He understands our pain,
not pity because He has never experienced hurt.*

40

joy and sadness can be felt together

Monday, May 21, 2018: We continued to count our blessings as John was more awake and alert as the time went on. And John was more and more excited that the doctors decided to extubate him as the intubation tube was the fundamental thorn in his side on top of everything else he was facing after being admitted to the hospital. He wanted to breathe on his own. He begged the doctors to let him breathe on his own. And he wanted to talk—no shock there. He's a Benbow.

John wasted no time using his newfound voice to poke fun at anything and everything, starting right out of the gate with the idea that my sister and I looked "like crap."

First of all, rude. We joked back that we had been up for almost three days straight because "someone" had decided to get into an accident. I told him there were other ways to see me again after the wedding. He smiled and then he said that he hadn't slept either.

Ummmm, I am not familiar with the ins and outs of medical procedures, but I joked back by saying, "you just had an eight-hour back reconstruction surgery. I am pretty sure you slept."

His eyes widened to that familiar ornery look that we all know too well.

"I did?!"

Slight pause.

Then he coughed up something even more ornery. He thought he was so funny. My sister and I laughed and laughed. John did too. And then he grabbed his abdomen as the motion of laughing started causing pain somewhere on the inside that he wasn't able to pinpoint due to the paralysis.

We stopped laughing. Instead we talked about something else.

At first he tried comforting us. Did you catch that? He tried comforting us. Of course, it wasn't very comforting as he tried to tell us about his belief in quantum suicide and rebirth. He insisted

42

that all would be fine because "in your reality I die, but in mine I live again."

Cool, John. I believe that we get to live again too but without the whole ruling our own galaxy thing. That still doesn't mean that I want you to go. Can't we just keep talking about how you jokingly asked if they did any body modifications while you were under or about how you complemented the good looks of one of your nurses and then mistook her for another nurse less than an hour later for the one you attempted flirting with? Because that was the brother I wanted to talk to. Even though he said the most embarrassing things.

Hard pass on the death stuff bro, hard pass.

We were incredibly fortunate that despite his mortifying list of injuries, John still had his wits about him. Monday was a testament to that as he slept on and off and enjoyed all manners of conversation with those visiting. One visitor in particular had showed up the night before and instantly made me feel at home. When I saw my husband Rich walk through the hospital doors, I could physically feel the stress and anxiety leave my body. Everything was going to be okay, I told myself. Well, okay was the understatement of the century as John continued to be visibly frustrated with his limbs not responding how he wanted them to and feeling had yet to return to the abdomen he was casually pushing on, but he was alive. He was going to make it.

My brother wasn't out of the woods yet and we knew that, but everyone looked pretty ragged, and I knew that my husband had a lot of work to get back to so I thought it best to send everyone home on Monday night. Rich back to the coast to take care of our boys and the church after a quick twenty-four-hour trip and my family back to their homes all scattered around the area no more than forty-five minutes away. We all needed one good night of sleep, and they all had warm beds that could make that happen.

My parents especially did not like this plan. I understood as my brother intended to rent their home after their move so even though their bed was still in the house they had just left, John's stuff was also there. I pushed for them to leave anyway. It wasn't benefiting anyone, especially John, if we all ran ourselves into the ground. He was getting better; they could get some rest. That was that. And so they left.

I pulled out my blanket, my bible, my headphones, and a pillow and set up shop beside his bed. He was supposed to sleep. He never did.

Don't get me wrong, he tried to sleep. But with everything going on, he could never really settle down. Also there was the constant beeping from the machines and poking and prodding from the nurses. I get it. It was all too much.

We talked for a few minutes, but having been in the hospital for over fifty-six hours at that point, most of which were spent with family, he was over having to talk. Mainly because his throat was so raw from being intubated that it made him sound like a hoarse pubescent boy... but also because our family can hold our own in a small talk competition. I needed a little pause from talking myself and welcomed his suggestion of listening to music.

He asked for a band that I wasn't familiar with, and I quickly looked through iTunes Music to download their albums. At first he resisted telling me that he was "being selfish" by wanting to listen to "his music" as he knew I had kept my music folders strictly to Christian bands for my own reasons, but I told him not to be silly.

"As long as there are no curse words or sexually explicit lyrics, [his] music would be just fine," I remember saying.

Tame Impala. That's who he asked for. A techno band that I had never heard of. But I was always up for a good beat, so I typed their name in the search bar. The Internet was slower than molasses in that concrete building, so we listened to one song three times on repeat before I realized that nothing else was loading.

Halfway through the "Let it Happen" marathon (*yes that was the name of the only song that loaded and played*), a nurse walked in. A woman I had never seen in that hospital in all of the time we had spent there. Truth is, I never saw her again after that one time. I like to think to myself that she was some sort of angel. Her radiantly black skin that glistened off of the fluorescent lights now set to dim and her smile that stretched from ear to ear matched the beauty that poured out of her. Just her presence in the room was like joy itself had stepped in. Which was ironic as she was there to clean John's mouth with what was essentially a small sponge at the end of a sucker stick which hurt to no end. The nurses had to scrub his mouth as hard as they could to keep his injuries clean. It was painful even to watch, so I was glad the music was playing to fill the would-be quiet void to hopefully keep him distracted long enough to get it over with.

As she entered she looked directly at me, giving pause to her duties. And then with a smirk and a tilt of the head responding to the techno music she heard coming from my phone, she danced.

She quite literally bounced and bopped her way into the room.

I got a kick at the sight of her waltzing over to my brother's bed, hands raised in the air. This woman danced across the floor, and for a moment I forgot how serious everything was. I forgot the reason my brother was in that hospital bed or that he couldn't move anything from the waist down. I forgot... and I danced too.

My brother, who was supposed to be resting, joined in by lifting his hands in rhythm to the song. For that one minute, time stood still and there was laughter instead of sorrow. Everything seemed right in the world. It came just as quickly as it went.

The song ended, she scrubbed his mouth, and then she left the room. I chuckled a bit as she went, making sure to make eye contact with her on the way out as if to say "thank you" despite the words escaping me. She nodded as if she knew.

Hours passed of juggling, trying to get a sponge of water for my brother to locating his "vacuum spit sucker thing" for clearing out his mouth. He insisted he do it himself as the intubation tube and nurses had traumatized him by having anyone near his throat, the uvula in particular. I kid you not—I will never be able to hear "uvula" the same again as he complained to every family member that Monday about one nurse in particular that "punctured [his] uvula" causing us to have to check it for him every few hours for bleeding and swelling. We laughed until our sides hurt.

There were a few snags throughout the night that caused lingering concerns—like his not being able to cough. It sounded like he was saying the word cough or "cuuhk" rather than being able to actually do it, and there was this one time that he panicked as I had briefly fallen asleep and he was unable to locate the vacuum spit sucker. But when my father showed up a little before 5 am the next morning, I was relieved as it meant that it I wouldn't have to be on guard and could stop fighting my body that so desperately wanted to rest.

I smiled as I left, seeing John finally at peace and comfortable. I hugged my father while still giving him all the side eye for not sleeping in longer and then wandered into the secret second waiting room that we had only just discovered Sunday night as there were two recliners and a couch that I could sink into. And sink I did.

- - - - - - - -

This part of the story is my favorite. Not only because of our one dance, the last we would ever share, but because it was filled to the brim with joy despite the sadness, instead of just sadness. I have always thought that these two things could not fit into the same circumstance together, but I was wrong. I have ventured through these last nine months with both. They walk the road together.

This could seem nonsensical if you take these two words at

face value likening them to each other in a way where one cancels the other out—but that is where I had missed it too. They are not the same. One is an emotional response, while the other is a choice. And we can both choose joy while still responding with sadness without negating or taking value from either one.

As a youth pastor for many years, I was gifted the opportunity to speak to teenage girls in many different formats, my favorite was always in the self-image or character-building settings. One year in particular I thought I would be especially "hip and in with it" and used a play on words. The phrase, *What the What*. In all honesty, it was a phrase that I used more than that younger generation, and it was funny all the same. And to make it stick, I took each word and broke it down, relating it to the most powerful thing that they were facing in their lives. (The same powerful thing that we all face.)

Our *feelings*.

They are the most powerful because they have the ability to change everything. I can't speak for you, but when I am emotionally wound up about something, I don't always think rationally. If I see a person of any age being harsh with one of my sons, it's not just Momma Bear that comes out but a whole lot of crazy too. And while I strongly respect and uphold the Ten Commandments in my daily life, I will give no second thought to murdering any woman who even looks at my husband with a twinkle in her eye. Why? Because of feelings. Unrestrained, pure illogical, *feelings*.

Will I act on these? Of course not. Will I dream about acting on them? Possibly. Because there is no way to *not* feel them. And in the in-between phase of feeling and responding, there is a vital process we must go through to make sure that those pesky little reactors don't set off a chain reaction of dominoes that end up causing even more destruction in our life. Because they can. And sometimes I am too caught up in it all to care. Until life settles and I care very much.

47

I believe I have shared that my natural inclination in emergency situations is to go numb. This isn't because I have somehow found the valve and willfully shut it off, but rather a survival instinct that kicks in. It's helpful in most scenarios, until it's not. Like the time I convinced myself that because feelings were "bad," I shouldn't have them and decided instead to float emotionless through life. I. Was. Wrong. Feelings are not the enemy.

Are we wrong for having them? Is it ok for a Christian to be sad? Is it ok to cry? Is it ok to grieve for more than forty days? (God bless the well-meaning woman who pointed out this beautiful grief timeline from Middle Eastern culture. Forgive her Lord; she knows not what she does.)

The more I thought about this topic, the more I couldn't help but think: we were *created* to have emotions.

Jesus had emotions. He was angry when He turned over the tables in the temple, He was sad when He heard of his friend's death, and He was lonely when He felt God's presence leave Him on the cross. Having the emotion? Not sin. Using that emotion to hurt others or yourself? Congratulations you have joined the rest of humanity in sinning which is why God saw it fit to separate feelings from action when He inspired the words found in Ephesians 4:26, "be angry and do not sin."

I get it, separating the two is tricky. Because sometimes the only thing that sounds good is a full-blown tantrum, trying to figure out how to toss tables like Jesus and still be considered pure. Because life hurts and it causes the deepest of wounds. And you are not wrong and absolutely justified for hurting the way you are. But there has to be more than just feelings—we have to train ourselves how to make good choices too.

We can be justified in feeling offended, but choose not to gossip.

We can be justified in feeling lonely, but choose not to dive into an impure or abusive relationship.

We can be justified in feeling depressed, but choose not to allow ourselves to withdraw from life.

We can be justified in feeling deep sadness, but choose not to live in sorrow.

We can be justified. I know.

Sometimes this world is stormy and dark. I don't talk about these things being myself unscathed by the "cosmic powers over this present darkness" that it talks about in Ephesians 6. I don't assume we can "buck up little buckaroo" and just find somewhere deep inside ourselves to pull strength out of and press on. Remember, it's not there. We can't do it.

But God.

We can't do this. But God can.

Our Good Father gives us the strength to choose the right things when we feel like choosing the wrong ones. He infuses life into our dry bones and replaces our weakness for strength. Through Him and only through Him can we feel rejection, but choose love, or feel grief but choose joy. Both still being very present.

I am not the master at this. I am not even an expert in the field. But what I can tell you is that I have used that silly phrase over and over again in my life to combat letting sadness completely overwhelm me. I can tell you that sitting beside my brother as I watched him blow less and less into the tube to gauge his lung capacity that I had to continually choose to separate what I was feeling from what I would say in response. Because it was not good. It was terrible. And I knew what it meant. I knew something was wrong.

But instead of freaking out, we danced.

I want this for us. You and I in our tough spots. I want us to dance in the rain and laugh through our tears. Not because we should be callous and unfeeling, but because we are willing and able to what-the-what our situations all day until our circumstances change or our feelings do. I am still visiting my brother's memorial bench and crying over men that look like him. I am still turning my head when a television show includes an accident scene or cringe when a motorcycle passes me by. And I still hold my breath when holidays come and go and family gathers without him in the room. Despite my feelings or my circumstances changing, you will still find me cackling with my outrageous laugh in some corner somewhere as I recount another bad mom move or trip over my own two feet. And that is ok too.

So what exactly does that little phrase that I have held onto for so long actually provoke us to do? They are merely questions to ask yourself in tough times. But they work. I promise they work.

What am I feeling?

Put a name on it. The first step to any recovery is labeling the issue. So what is it exactly that you are feeling? It has a name. Fear is a name, grief is a name, rejection is a name, abandonment is a name, and the list goes on. It is ok to say "I feel angry" as long as you recognize that you are feeling it and not acting on it. "I feel angry" is very different from attaching it to your identity and saying "I am angry."

The reason is...

Understand that there are real circumstances for why you feel the way you do. They are valid. You are not a terrible person for having this emotion. In fact, I am so, so sorry that you do. I am sorry not for the feeling but for the reason you are feeling it. For the argument or the altercation or the abuse or the death. I am sorry.

Lift your head up and allow yourself to feel. God does not expect you to be a robot. Talk through what happened, but then don't stop there! Don't get into the circle of only asking your-self "what the" and never getting to the last "what." That is how we get ourselves into trouble, only focusing on our feelings and what happened to us. Besides, nothing good ever comes after "what the...."

What does the Bible say?

This is the last and most important question. It is the source of strength and the very reason we can praise before our breakthrough.

Allow me to go on a little nerd side trail for a minute. In the *Lord of the Rings*, there is a scene where Gandalf the White is standing on the bridge holding out his staff to guard Frodo Baggins so he can escape with the ring that is crucial to everyone's survival, without being attacked. The camera pulls away to reveal to the audience hundreds of creatures charging toward Gandalf while Frodo safely makes his passage but not before Gandalf makes this one declarative statement that changes everything.

He shouts to the enemy, "You shall not pass!"

I love this scene. I could not love this scene more.

Because I feel it in my bones. I want to stand on my couch and yell with him, *you shall not pass*, although in doing so I am pretty sure I would scare my two boys and a few dogs too. But this image is so powerful. You see, Gandalf is like the Word that keeps guard over our hearts and minds. When offense, hatred, loneliness, lust, depression, or any other feeling you face tries to lay root in your heart, Gandalf (the Word) rises up and says "You shall not pass."

Not this heart. Not today. I know it hurts right now, but God is faithful and will see me through this.

The Bible says in Proverbs 4:23 that we are to "guard our heart above all else for out of it flows the springs of life." This can seem daunting because the Bible also says that our hearts are "deceitfully wicked who can know it?" (Jeremiah 17:9). But it is not impossible! Because we are not the ones in charge of guarding it. The very small Frodo was not left alone on the bridge to fight off the enemy and try to escape with the ring. No, he had help, and so do we!

Let's look at this passage from Psalm 119 *(sidenote: it is the longest chapter in the entire Bible and the only one with 176 verses devoted to one theme—the Word being light to our paths)*:

> How can a young man keep his way pure? By guarding it according to your word. With my whole heart I seek you; let me not wander from your commandments! I have stored up your word in my heart, that I might not sin against you. Blessed are you, O Lord; teach me your statutes! With my lips I declare all the rules of your mouth. In the way of your testimonies I delight as much as in all riches. I will meditate on your precepts and fix my eyes on your ways. I will delight in your statutes; I will not forget your word.
>
> (Psalm 119: 9–16)

The key we find in this Scripture is that the Word is not just a guide but also a guard!

If you don't know what the Word says, then you are left defenseless for an attack. You are allowing passage for the very enemy of your soul to tear you down piece by piece, one feeling-led action to another. No one wakes up wanting to commit murder, adultery, or suicide; they allow one thought, one feeling, to fester too long and do something that they can never take back.

Let it not be so with us! We have too many resources at our fingertips to suffer without knowing what the Word says to do because this world will have other ideas. Just think of the phrase "follow your heart" and you will understand how wrong that can go when our heart is broken or outraged. Plus there is the whole idea that you cannot physically follow and guard something at the same time.

It is therefore imperative that you find what the Bible says about your situation. And if you can't seem to find anything on your own, phone a friend or a pastor to help you in your search or use "the" Google (just make sure to use a credible source like biblegateway.com or bible.com to prevent from wrong information).

Friend, please know that you're feelings are real and they happen for a reason, but they will also lead you down a path with no good ending. Guard them. Above all else. And God will see you through.

Finally, be strong in the Lord and in the strength of His might. Put on the whole armor of God, that you may be able to stand against the schemes of the devil. For we do not wrestle against flesh and blood, but against the rulers, against the authorities, against the cosmic powers over this present darkness, against the spiritual forces of evil in the heavenly places. Therefore take up the whole armor of God, that you may be able to withstand in the evil day, and having done all, to stand firm.

(EPHESIANS 6:10-13)

if you are tired and weary from giving it all you've got all the time. if you don't have any fight left. just keep standing. Standing is still winning.

asking for help is better than going it alone

Tuesday, May 22, 2018: I woke up on Tuesday morning after a short three-hour nap to the news that my brother's condition was declining and a tube had to be reinserted to help his lungs breath and heal. The updates were not great but they weren't terrible either. John would be okay, but he had a lot more to overcome. The constant yo-yoing back and forth had me more nauseous than any other day before as uneasiness with the outcome came crawling into our waiting room.

My cousin Brad who had shown up at the hospital on the day my brother was brought in as he was local to the area spent as much time as possible after work and family responsibilities with us. Every time I saw him come through the door, my heart rested for a moment. He had my brother's humor and made me feel like a piece of him was present, untouched by this tragedy.

Brad even pulled a total big brother move by poking fun at the outfit that I had on that day. In his defense, it was a large baggy maroon sweater coupled with a pair of maroon skinny jeans. I get it. He wasn't wrong when he said that I looked like a professional ice skater when he spotted me earlier in the parking lot. But when you are packing under duress, you don't care if you have "enough" clothes or even if they are "fashionably appropriate" clothes. You just need clothes. Any clothes. Even a coordinating maroon sweater and pant set. That'll do.

It wasn't just the outfit. I looked like a total buffoon that Tuesday night. By this time I had yet to leave the hospital, and when my mother said that she needed to get out to pick up a few burgers for the family, I offered to join her without hesitation. It had been almost four days without a full meal, which disappointed me not at all as my hunger had still not returned, but my clothes were fitting a little looser than usual.

Anxiety weight loss. It's a real thing.

As we exited the hospital, I felt my head being jerked to the left by a small patch of hair caught underneath my purse strap. I opted to move the purse from one shoulder to the other instead of yanking on the hair preventing further pain, and in doing so the most important thing fell off of my boney, unfed fingers.

My ring.

Not the one I had fallen in love with and purchased in Lebanon to replace the wedding ring given to me by my husband. Not the promise ring I had received thirteen years ago from Rich, my then boyfriend. No, this ring was something else entirely. It was the ring that my brother had given me less than a month before as he attempted to purge a few items left from his soon-to-be divorce.

This ring, the tiny white gold band lined with sapphire diamonds, had been sitting in his drawer too small for anyone in our family to wear. When I had visited last, he asked if I wore jewelry and if I had wanted it, to which I gladly accepted. Mainly because it was from him, and despite our living five hours apart, he has an incredibly special place in my heart. But also because my mother has always wore a ring on her knuckle and being that this tiny ring wouldn't look right on my pinky, it would mimic my mother's by resting halfway up on my middle finger. His favorite finger, no less.

Now that you understand its significance especially amid our current situation, can you feel the anguish that was in my heart when I felt it slip off of my hand? Can you imagine the inner turmoil as I dropped to my knees to scour the ground for this delicate piece of metal that meant more to me than any other gift I had ever received up to this point?

Also, I lost the ring right in front of my mother who is one of the most sentimental human beings to walk this earth, which is beautiful, and equally terrifying when your severely ill brother is lying in a hospital bed and the one thing you have been given by said brother is hiding somewhere in a very public outdoor space which may or may not ever be recovered.

I was heartbroken.

Thankfully I had saved the truly desperate actions for after I had sent my mother along noting that Bethany's new father-in-law Carl would be arriving at any moment with a metal detector to help in the search.

Yes I did use a metal detector in a public hospital parking lot. In my super awesome outfit and all. I. Did. Not. Care. And hence, received a wonderful picture of an ice skater in a very closely related outfit a few hours later from my cousin. Thanks, Brad.

When Bethany's father-in-law arrived, I was relieved. I had kept a small amount of composure around my mother so as to not allow more undue stress on top of everything else, knowing that having an actual metal detector would give us a fighting chance. Until that little thing beeped at anything in sight. Literally *anything*. The sidewalk, the curb, the flowers... anything. With each passing moment, my once calm demeanor determined to find this missing piece of jewelry turned to one of frantic mania that caused me to dig up every plant bed that once neatly bordered the walking path on the edge of a complete breakdown.

In that moment of toiling and utter frustration, I was so thankful for Carl, my fellow "archaeologist," who was an incredibly patient man. He never walked away, never told me to throw in the towel, and never looked down on the way I was choosing to look for the thing I had lost. Even if it meant digging up a bush or two. Or ten. Don't judge. This is a no-judgment zone. In fact, Carl rolled up his sleeves and dug up a few himself.

After about an hour of searching which of course felt like an eternity, I was at the point of giving up. I stood to my feet and let my tear-filled eyes wander to the patch of cement directly in front of me when I caught a glimpse of something. My heart raced and I lunged forward. It was here all along, in the middle of the path hidden by the small yellow bumps meant to alert pedestrians of upcoming traffic crossing.

I had found it!

I clutched the ring with both hands and collapsed onto the

pavement, sobbing the whole way down. Carl joined me by sitting on the curb. His voice was calm and peaceful as he attempted to tell me that everything was going to be alright. John would get better, and we would figure things out.

His words didn't sound patronizing, but they also didn't settle as true. "John has an infection," I stated through my tears. "He is getting worse, not better."

"Infections are common. The doctors are treating him and he is getting excellent care," he repeated back to me. I could hear the compassion in his voice and the concern he had for my brother, but after the things we experienced and all of the daunting reports from doctors day after day, there was no pulling me out of it. I clutched the ring, he helped me up, and we went back inside where Brad was waiting to tell everyone about my little adventure.

Bless his heart.

- - - - - - - -

Community is a funny thing when you mix in situations of loss. There may never be a point where we decide to push away from society all together, but that doesn't mean that every social gathering thereafter isn't in some way affected. Because it is. Everything is.

In the beginning of my journey with grief, I struggled to engage with my friends and even some extended family due to our vastly different experiences with John's death. Some knew my brother at a distance, some were close but connected through different interests, and still others had not known him at all. Whatever their own link, it was not my own and it felt obscure to hear words about him coming from what I imagined to be an insincere place. They didn't sound as bothered, as destroyed really, by his passing. But of course I wasn't firing at all cylinders and told myself to stop being so nonsensical. Of course they were sad. They were just sad in a different way.

All of these emotions of feeling "more in pain" by those I was surrounded by caused me to start a mass exodus into my own little world.

Why hadn't anyone called?

Why wasn't anyone still talking about him?

Who could understand my pain?

All of my questions piled up and before I knew it, it was just me and Jesus. My grief had caused further and further isolation. And I was happy to let it sweep me away. I was convinced that no one understood.

This is where the lesson learned in Chapter 2 became ever so apparent in my life. The idea that others were experiencing their own kinds of losses and pains made me feel less like a victim and more like a human sharing in the very real human experience of suffering. Something our Savior is not unfamiliar with.

I like to think back to His time in the garden of Gethsemane when He was under excruciating pressure—a sadness He likened to death—and decided to bring three of His closest friends with Him to pray. The story is a perfect depiction of what I was feeling. This is what the Scriptures record in Matthew's account:

Then Jesus went with them to a place called Gethsemane, and he said to his disciples, 'Sit here, while I go over there and pray.' And taking with him Peter and the two sons of Zebedee, he began to be sorrowful and troubled. Then he said to them, 'My soul is very sorrowful, even to death; remain here, and watch with me.' And going a little farther he fell on his face and prayed, saying, 'My Father, if it be possible, let this cup pass from me; nevertheless, not as I will, but as you will.' And he came to the disciples and found them sleeping. And he said to Peter, 'So, could you not watch with me one hour? Watch and pray that you may not enter into temptation. The spirit indeed is willing, but the flesh is weak.' Again, for the second time, he went away and prayed, 'My Father, if this cannot pass unless I drink it, your will be done.' And again he came and found them sleeping, for their eyes were heavy. So, leaving them again, he went away and prayed for the third time, saying the same words again. Then he came to the disciples and said to them, 'Sleep and take your rest later on. See, the hour is at hand, and the Son of Man is betrayed into the hands of sinners. Rise, let us be going; see, my betrayer is at hand.'

(MATTHEW 26: 36–46)

Jesus was interceding and speaking to God with desperation for the journey that God was leading Him on, and three times He found His friends asleep. They just didn't get it.

I feel this. To the core of my being I feel this.

It isn't because they were evil or bad friends or choosing to be ignorant of the circumstances around them. It could have been that they had never been in that position before. The Bible never records the disciples walking with someone through this great of a spiritual opposition and eminent death. It is not too far off to believe that they most likely just didn't understand.

This belief that you are alone even among friends in the dark roads you face can be debilitating. You might be tempted to throw away years of friendship or quit a job over it; there is no limit really to what we are capable of feeling. *(Insert a big dose of what-the-what here to stay calm and not cause more chaos than we are already facing.)*

I encourage you in this, my friend, to fight that urge.

I am not much of an aggressive person. In fact, anything that involves a fight or two opposing forces with built-up emotion causes me to flee for the hills. In the fight, flight, or freeze responses, I would fall mainly in the last two categories without hesitation. However, this doesn't mean that I could not carry my own if absolutely necessary. If my kids are involved and for some reason I have the blessing of the Lord, this momma will throw down. I have learned a few things along the way that would ensure my victory. Just trust that.

The most important piece of advice of fighting I have found is this: Unless you are Jack Bauer, you should never be caught alone. *And honestly even Jack had backup. They were just in a different city when he was facing opposition.*

Being alone is a sure fire way of getting into trouble. That is why Jesus went to pray. To pull God's presence and protection into His life. Even though it turned out that God's will was leading Him directly into the enemies' hands and not away from them. Which is another chapter altogether. But this is also why He brought a few friends.

We are going to face problems of all sizes. The Bible literally guarantees it. Jesus Himself spoke to the disciples in John 16 near the end of His ministry by saying:

> Behold, the hour is coming, indeed it has come, when you will be scattered, each to his own home, and will leave me alone. Yet I am not alone, for the Father is with me. I have said these things to you, that in me you may have peace. In the world you will have tribulation. But take heart; I have overcome the world.
>
> (VERSES 32–33)

This challenge to "take heart" came from a place of sincerity and honesty. It was not a "suck it up" mantra but one of understanding and care. He knew that His friends would feel alone, like they failed, and abandoned. He knew they would face persecution and even death. But Jesus paved the way and was the example of how to face such tragedies. With God… and with people.

Ask yourself these two questions:

When was the last time you prayed about your situation and invited God into the middle of it?

This is not meant to provoke condemnation. I want you to take a real assessment of the last time you stopped and asked for the Holy Spirit's company. For Him to join you on your quest to recover what was stolen or lost or damaged on the way. Even if some of it cannot be found. He is after all an "ever-present help in time of need."

As I was wading through the bushes that day at the hospital, I was so thankful to have someone like Carl who had the tools needed to locate such a treasured gift. Without his company and the now understood misplaced trust I had in his rinky-dink machine, I would have never made it to the point of success. I would have given up. Because alone I was not prepared and ready for what I was facing.

The Holy Spirit is way more capable of handling our losses than we will ever be. He is not a faulty metal detector that is confused on what constitutes an actual piece of metal but in fact a Comforter, a Counselor, and a Friend. One who understands what it is to lose "my brother" because in all of John's wanderings from the Lord, he had lost fellowship with him first. And my God loves my brother more than I ever could. He created Him, so it was painful for Him, too.

I love this about Him. God understood loss in many forms. Jesus experienced the loss of friendships when Judas betrayed Him, the loss of support when the disciples turned their backs, and the loss of hope in His preferred outcome when God answered that He had to die. From the Father's perspective, He had to walk through even more losses as he endured the loss of normalcy and community when He sent His Son to the earth, the loss of a relationship when He had to turn His presence from His Son on the cross, and the loss of life when He watched Jesus die.

God knows loss.

In fact He was just as desperate in His journey to regain connection with a lost humanity as I was in my search for the ring. Caring not at all if a few bushes were torn up in the process. I can imagine His desperation because I know how it felt to feel desperate for John. Thinking how my ring may have been too lost, too far gone, to be discovered just how my brother might have been to God. I think of my time in the landscape as the woman looking for her lost coin in Luke Chapter 15. I can guarantee you that no piece of furniture was left untouched in the process of her seeking to find what could not, for the moment, be found. Because she would have done anything, I would have done anything, to find that ring and for God to find my brother. And God, He knows just how desperate this feels.

Not only does He understand the urgency, but He also isn't going to beat you over the head if you invite Him into your mess, telling you to get over it or stop crying. He will sit with you on a curb in the middle of a parking lot reminding you of the truths in your situation with hope, comfort, kindness, and peace. He gets it.

Jesus invited His Father in when He dedicated a time to pray for Him and seek Him. But He didn't stop there. He invited others along also (despite their consistently falling asleep). Which is the second thing we have to ask ourselves.

Who am I letting into the pilgrimage of grief with me?

I know that it doesn't always feel comfortable. I get that you are a strong, capable, independent man or woman. I am too. But doing it alone is not God's idea of being strong, capable, or independent. Pushing others away will only solidify greater pain and struggle. And friend, we both know that you don't need any more than you already are facing.

This battle you face is yours alone, which is true. You are the one that has to face the ugliness of life after it has been marred and broken. But God has never asked that you face it by yourself. He knew it would be too great a task.

When God called Moses to lead the Israelites out of Egypt, he wasn't just asking him to lead them on a long walk. He was asking Moses to fight against every enemy that would come against them, and there were many. He was asking Moses to look beyond their sin, look beyond their complaining, look beyond their rebellion, and fight for them. Fight for them because he was the only one who was promised victory.

He was the only one.

In Exodus 17:8–16, we find Moses instructing Joshua to lead the army to battle as he would stand on Mt. Sinai with his arms raised. This was how God instructed Moses that they would win; Joshua would fight and Moses would stand with his hands to the heavens.

> Then Amalek came and fought with Israel at Rephidim. So Moses said to Joshua, 'Choose for us men, and go out and fight with Amalek. Tomorrow I will stand on the top of the hill with the staff of God in my hand.' So Joshua did as Moses told him, and fought with Amalek, while Moses, Aaron, and Hur went up to the top of the hill.
>
> (Exodus 17:8–10)

At first glance it sounds like Moses got the better end of the staff, so to speak, but have you ever tried holding your arms up for any length of time? I have... it was one of our punishments as a kid. We had to stand in a corner with our hands above our heads for however long a time period that matched our disobedience. *I would love to meet the person who gave my father that idea. It hurts. But I digress.*

As long as Moses' hands were raised, they would win, but he

grew tired as anyone would, and his arms that once weighed only a few pounds now felt like he was carrying the literal weight of the world. And as his arms sank lower to the ground, the armies sank lower to the Amalekites.

Only Moses' hands would earn their victory.

Only his. Aaron (Moses' brother) could do no good with his arms flailing in the air begging for God to give the battle to him—it was not his battle to fight. But reading further into Scripture, we find that Aaron could "do" something. He could do one thing. He could hold up the arms of Moses. He could support him.

Because even though Moses had to do it himself, he did not have to do it alone.

Whenever Moses held up his hand, Israel prevailed, and whenever he lowered his hand, Amalek prevailed. But Moses' hands grew weary, so they took a stone and put it under him, and he sat on it, while Aaron and Hur held up his hands, one on one side, and the other on the other side. So his hands were steady until the going down of the sun. And Joshua overwhelmed Amalek and his people with the sword.

(EXODUS 17:11–13)

We all need a few Aarons and Hurs in our lives. We need people to walk beside us as we figure it out. We need friends with shovels and work clothes to go on a grand expedition with us as we find our hope and joy again. And we need people with smartphones to take pictures of ice skaters to send to us later to remind us of just how desperate we might have looked while doing it, but all in good fun. Because we need to laugh a little, too.

Find someone to help hold your arms up, someone who will support you no matter their personal understanding of your circumstances or their personal connection to it, and someone who will let you feel safe feeling and acting a little desperate and hopeless as you journey back to being fully known and found.

I one hundred percent support grief counseling and counseling in all forms, but I also believe in the power of friendship. This should not be a one or the other situation. We need both. And especially friends who will challenge you to keep doing right when you get tired and weak, who will remind you to think and speak the Word over your situation, and who will stand with you believing God for your victory.

Give us those people, Lord!

And not just that, but make us those people Lord. Because there will come a day when we are given the chance to be that friend.

I love that in the letters to the Corinth church, Paul challenges the believers who have been through trials to use those experiences to help others facing similar struggles. Essentially he asks us to "pay it forward." Because no one understands a widow like a widow, or an orphan like an orphan, or a hate crime survivor like a hate crime survivor. You will one day be the answered prayer that someone has been believing for because you have walked through the darkness yourself. You will be able to understand more than anyone how to offer support knowing that you may be able to do nothing but "be there," but that "being there" is enough.

Someone is going to need you. But until you find your way into the light of a new day yourself, I pray you find the one who has gone before you or the one who is willing to dig up a few bushes if it is what you need.

Blessed be the God and Father of our Lord Jesus Christ,

paying it forward

the Father of mercies and God of all comfort, who

comforts us in all our affliction, so that we may be able

to comfort those who are in any affliction, with the

comfort with which we ourselves are comforted by God.

For as we share abundantly in Christ's sufferings, so

through Christ we share abundantly in comfort too.

'abundantly in comfort'. I love that

(2 CORINTHIANS 1: 3-5)

68

it is okay to wrestle

Wednesday, May 23, 2018: John was getting progressively worse. I called my husband to keep him informed of the updates, kicking myself for even letting him go home in the first place, but there was nothing any of us could do. That Wednesday morning during my first call, Rich told me about a vivid dream that he had dreamt the night before. He said that he was looking into John's hospital room, and my father and I were praying with him as he acknowledged the existence of God in his life. My chest tightened as I thought about all of the missed opportunities I might have had up until this point only to have realized the urgency now when John was almost completely sedated, nearing the line between life and death.

An hour or two later, I found myself sitting by John's bedside and talking to him about heaven. I gathered my composure the best I could and told John that I knew he was still holding on to his science-based belief in an afterlife but that I was praying for God to show Himself as true through whatever means necessary.

I imagined the two of them, God and John, sitting down and talking for hours while he was in this current state allowing my brother to ask all of the hard questions that he had built up over the years. I imagined my brother being cynical and feisty with his interrogating of God's goodness, character, and very existence while God remained patient and wise and loving. I imagined God looking upon John with kind eyes and allowing my brother to be his most raw self but never changing His response to him. I prayed that this was what was happening. I begged the Lord to be pleading with John the way I wanted to plead but was still so unsure if I would ruin his idea of religion because of me.

This has always been my fear. Being known solely as a pastor's wife making no room for anything other than being a pillar of faith at all times. Crying and yelling were not allowed, I thought, as I bore the sole example of religion to those burned by it most. Both in our family and out of it. The only problem was that *I am not Jesus*, and my family and those closest to us had a front row seat to watch my humanity in all of its forms.

I ruined them. I ruined their ever knowing God. That's what I believed. What I still fight believing. And it is because of this personalization about their hurts and offenses through the church that I was desperate to be perfect so that they would see Christ in me and somehow find their way back. I have never wanted anything more than people to find their way back. This is the sole reason I decided that God must have been right when He called me into the ministry. Not because I was polished and spotless, but because I was desperate to see a generation reconciled back to Him. Despite my shortcomings.

After I spoke into John's ear about heaven, the room became increasingly hurried. Nurses flooded in and out, machines were beeping, and I was rushed out into the hall to join what family I had there. This was bad. I knew down deep in my gut something had shifted and we might just lose him after all.

We stood helplessly by while my brother was moved from one section of the building to another section with larger rooms for him to be placed in a special bed that rotated 360 degrees to drain the fluid from every orifice of his body. As they pushed his hospital bed past us in the hall, my family made sure to stay out of the way but speak loud enough for John to hear us—if there were any chance he could hear us at all.

We told him that we loved him. That he was a fighter. That we wouldn't leave until he was okay. And then the doors closed behind the barrage of nurses and hospital staff, leaving us to wait again in that darn waiting room. The one I had now come to hate. We waited for the news that he was settled and we could go back in to sit with him. We waited for a long time.

A few minutes went by. And then a few more. Then an hour. We paced, we cried, and we silently held on to whatever strength we had left. And then the doctor returned. His eyes were not filled with hope. They weren't even reassuring. He told us that their team was struggling to stabilize John; his body hated the rotating bed, but he needed it for the infection to be drained from his lungs.

The doctor was honest, and brutal, with us.

He said that he didn't expect John to make it through the night.

John was going to die at any moment.

I swallowed hard and told myself to process what he had just said. That John was not going to make it through the night. How can this be right? *This was not right.*

In complete and utter anguish, I crumpled to the ground.

Rich was still at home. I had sent him home. We thought John was going to be okay, and he most certainly was not going to be okay. I had previously reasoned with myself that just talking to John about heaven was good enough. But now? Now they are saying he is going to die and I didn't pray the prayer? *I didn't pray the prayer.*

Brad sat next to me on the floor of the Trauma Neuro ICU hallway. I screamed a word over and over that would definitely not be acceptable to write in the context of which I was saying it. A word that I have not uttered in almost twenty years, and yet, in the moment, it was the only one that would escape my lips. My cousin just kept holding me and telling me how good God was. That John was good enough to make it, but I would not accept that. It is not who I have known God to be. Why make a way with the sacrifice of His own Son if being "good enough" would get you there?

I called Rich. I could barely get out words, but I still managed to say "He's dying. You need to come now."

Those words. I hated the way they tasted in my mouth, and I hated even more having to say them. I have been on the receiving end of that call when my mother-in-law couldn't get ahold of Rich in the middle of the night not even a year and a half prior to tell him that his younger brother had passed. I had to be the one to hear her relive the news she just received by the police officers at her door, and I had to be the one to call my husband to tell him this earth-shattering news. And now he would be the one to get the call. To hear my voice shriek as it filled with pain upon hearing that my younger brother too was going to die.

It felt like a cruel joke. My children had already lost one uncle, and now I would have to tell them that they were losing another. They were too young for this. We were too young for this.

This is where we scream at the heavens. This is where our pain seems too deep for God to comfort. This is where we want to die alongside the one we love because we cannot imagine, we cannot fathom, how we are supposed to just "move on" from here.

The doors swung open for any and all family members present, and without any order we rushed in to the area just outside of his new hospital room as we watched teams of medical staff do everything within their power to stabilize John. Every sound of his sats being too high or too low or too whatever confirmed his odds for not pulling through. And even though I had been sitting most of the day, I just couldn't stand any longer. I sat just outside of his door, watching one nurse walk around with a box of tissues to the nearly dozen people awaiting whatever horror we were about to experience. I made eye contact with her; her eyes were full of compassion.

"He's going to die, isn't he?" I asked.

"Yes." She paused. "He is."

I dropped my head and heard the footsteps of the chaplain and social worker join our anxiety-ridden group. I was mad. Angry. I can't really tell you why, but just the idea of hearing empty words of God's goodness when this woman had never lost a person so close felt repulsive. I assumed this of course because I dare not ask. I just looked up long enough to see her disconnected eyes to say that we didn't need a chaplain. That I was a pastor and we knew Jesus. I think I scared her off because she settled into the background after that.

Our eyes were glued to the window facing into John's room. It looked hopeless. It looked void of life. Stephanie, Harmony

(Stephanie's boyfriend), Bethany, Nolan, and I all started talking about what we would do if John would in fact pass away that night. It was an extension to the worst game my sister Stephanie and I have ever started to play just a day earlier, called "worst case scenario." We talked all about what we would do with his possessions, his funeral, and his life should the worst case happen. It seemed to be the right time to talk about it before we were knee deep in actual news of death when we were filled with sorrow or grief. This way we could talk about it like some hypothetical thing that was still far enough away to not feel like reality.

But this? There was no escaping this.

We had a front row seat to it.

Stephanie gathered the family into a corner of the large room where the nurse's station was placed. We all held hands as my sister, the one I had known from our childhood who showed me what it was like to be a Christian, led a prayer of peace and faith for our family. Asking for a miracle but also asking for comfort for our family if it was his time. I joined in the prayer and raised my own voice to God.

And then we waited for the outcome.

- - - - - - - -

I had grown to hate the waiting room as it was the physical representation of my growing anxieties. This room with the comfortable chairs no longer offered any comfort. And my family each shared the same disillusioned look in their eyes. It felt like a dream (read nightmare). It felt like at any moment, this cruel world would wake me from my slumber and I would be brought back to my usually unusual life along the coast. But alas the morning never came. Instead we lived in a perpetual state of darkness running to and fro and every which way in between wrestling with the worst of our questions and thoughts and ideas about the future that was unfolding.

Wrestling. It was exactly what it felt like. A long, drawn out match that exhausted both parties.

I don't do well with wrestling.

When my husband and I married in 2006, it came at a great shock to me to know that besides the understandable sporting events that would now grace our TV, a certain pretend wrestling show would also enter our home. I had never in my life watched an episode of WWE, and I can tell you with full confidence, I didn't like it. Not one bit. I am sure the people are nice enough, but wrestling has never and will never be something I am comfortable with.

The mixture between the close proximity you have with another human being and the amount of pure aggression displayed each "match" was enough to make my skin crawl. And don't even get me started on the sexualization of the women. Just don't.

I fought tooth and nail for my husband to stop watching it, but it was such a large part of his childhood and something that gave him an essence of nostalgia that we compromised instead with him recording and playing it while I was away from the house (skipping the girls in their skimpy clothing as he never watched that anyway).

"Wrestling. I. Hate. it."

When my husband and I found out that we were having our second child after having one boy already, we cheered. I just knew it would be a girl. I held on to the girl name that I had been saving since we married and prayed continually that God would give me this one thing. And then the ultrasound technician exclaimed that we were having a boy. I smiled enough. Was happy enough. And then when we reached the elevator, I cried. Big ugly embarrassing crocodile tears.

My husband reassured me that everything would be fine. We could try again or even adopt, but do you know what two boys would mean for our lives? Wrestling.

In our family there was one boy. And that poor kid would be found with glitter jellies and oversized shirts that looked like dresses because we were doing some kind of skit or game where John *had* to be a girl. Looking back it is a wonder that he didn't hate us or give us more protest.

When we told our families that we would be having another boy, my brother gave us an ecstatic "congratulations." My sisters understood the heartbreak I was facing, but John simply said, "now Michael has a brother. I always wanted a brother."

I knew what he meant. He didn't hate us or wish that he didn't have three sisters, he just always wondered what it would be like to not do what the girls wanted to do. I never saw it in him before, but it was a big deal for John. I wiped away my silly tears and welcomed quite the whirlwind of a child into our lives. A life that is now filled with loud arguing, physical altercations, and the sweetest exchange of brotherhood I have ever had the privilege to witness. I get it, John, brothers are the best.

But do you know what still isn't the best? Yes, wrestling.

I have always had a love–hate relationship with being in close proximity with anyone really. My mother had to comfort me as an inconsolable infant with my being face out, sitting on her knees. The feeling of being held that closely was in fact so excruciating for me that I squirmed with every hug (and especially every kiss), surprising my mother most of all when I decided to marry my high school sweetheart who happened to be four and a half years my senior and already a youth pastor at a mere twenty years old as it meant that "I would have to touch another person." You were right, mom. It is a little comical. Mainly because it does in fact take a lot of intentionality on my part.

Wrestling is the epitome of that struggle mainly as it involves two people battling strong emotions—and being pitted against each other. I am reminded of the imagery found in Scripture when Jacob wrestles with a man found in Genesis 32 believed to be God Himself. The fact that Jacob literally means "deceiver" or "grabber" comes at no surprise after reading his riddled past with his father, mother, and brother Esau. He lived up to his name in every sense and should have given me more of a clue when God insisted that our second-born son's name was going to be Jacob and not Paul. God most assuredly did not give us a Paul. We have a scrapper, that is for sure.

There are a few things about the story that I especially found connection with. It says:

> The same night he arose and took his two wives, his two female servants, and his eleven children, and crossed the ford of the Jabbok. He took them and sent them across the stream, and everything else that he had. And Jacob was left alone. And a man wrestled with him until the breaking of the day. When the man saw that he did not prevail against Jacob, he touched his hip socket, and Jacob's hip was put out of joint as he wrestled with him. Then he said, "Let me go, for the day has broken." But Jacob said, "I will not let you go unless you bless me." And he said to him, "What is your name?" And he said, "Jacob." Then he said, "Your name shall no longer be called Jacob, but Israel, for you have striven with God and with men, and have prevailed." Then Jacob asked him, "Please tell me your name." But he said, "Why is it that you ask my name?" And there he blessed him. So Jacob called the name of the place Peniel, saying, "For I have seen God face to face, and yet my life has been delivered." The sun rose upon him as he passed Penuel, limping because of his hip.
>
> (GENESIS 32:22–31)

Did you notice that Jacob sent his family on ahead of him? He was utterly alone. It was just him and his prayers as he prepared to meet with his brother Esau (who he had previously pulled a fast one on to gain his birthright).

He wasn't just alone, it was also the middle of the night. Complete darkness. This might be of no mention, but have you ever run into someone in the dark? I have. It's terrifying. It was also my dad who was waiting behind a door to scare me while I was trying to make my way to the bathroom. Needless to say, I didn't need to go to the bathroom anymore. If you are picking up what I am putting down.

What happens next is the stuff of my nightmares. A midnight wrestling match that lasts *all* night. Nothing but two strong-willed identities standing their ground in an all-out confrontation in the closest of quarters. Like I said. My nightmare.

In the end we find Jacob walking away with what he desired... and a limp. Some theologians believe that only God could have given the hip injury that he sustained as it only took a "touch" to come out of joint, and yet there is no mention of pain. The idea being that the exchange caused both a breaking and a healing leaving Jacob forever changed to walk through this world a little differently than before. Only God could have done this. But Jacob willingly entered the ring.

My sons, they would willingly enter the ring. My husband and all of his ten John Cena barbie dolls (ok action figures, and maybe they are my son's) gladly enter the ring.

But me? I do not want to go.

I want things to be nice and perfectly pinned up. I do not want to face the hard stuff, especially in such close quarters with the rest of my family who are equally hurting and frustrating and confused. I felt like I wanted to pull a Jacob and send everyone away so I could wrestle with my big questions in the darkness until He showed me why this needed to happen. Why it had to happen. Why my baby brother, my only brother, was not just facing paralysis but now death. *Now.* After miraculously surviving the accident, why now would this infection ravage his body?

The questions were mounting and I grew more and more

bothered by the inner turmoil. I am a pastor, am I even allowed to question God's presence or faithfulness? Because I was.

I felt like a failure on top of everything else going on. And then I felt something deep in my soul remind me of the real story behind the story of Jacob and his infamous wrestling match. God was not intimidated by his wanting to wrestle. God didn't just allow it to happen, but He engaged in it. Himself.

Jacob was not wrestling Jacob. Jacob was not even wrestling his questions. Jacob was wrestling with God. And He was big enough and secure enough and loving enough to let him wrestle. Because it is okay to battle the great unknown when we allow ourselves to battle it *with* a loving God and not without Him. That is our starting point. Our opponent if you will. Not our circumstances, not our questions, but the God of Abraham, Isaac, and Jacob Himself.

Start with Him. Allow yourself to take your anger and bitterness to Him to ask the hard questions. Now is not the time to venture out on your own or ask the hard questions to people who are not strong enough to bare them.

God doesn't think less of us or negate our life's purpose when we venture through dark seasons wondering if God is exactly who He says He is. He doesn't give up that easy.

One of my favorite passages in Scripture, in fact, is when Jesus is being faced with the worst thing He will ever face wanting God's will to change, knowing that He will be betrayed, and having to face his accusers when He had done nothing wrong but doing all of it knowing that His friends would *all* fall away. Literally all of them would deny Him. You might think that this would be a story about Jesus wrestling as He faces certain death, but the Scriptures highlight an entire group of solid believers who start journeying through doubt and denial of everything they thought they knew.

And Jesus allowed it.

Just read what He says to Peter when Jesus is explaining that the disciples would not stand firm in their faith when He would be crucified.

Jesus says:

'Simon, Simon, behold, Satan demanded to have you, that he might sift you like wheat, but I have prayed for you that your faith may not fail. And when you have turned again, strengthen your brothers.' Peter said to him, 'Lord, I am ready to go with you both to prison and to death.' Jesus said, 'I tell you, Peter, the rooster will not crow this day, until you deny three times that you know me.'

(LUKE 22:31–34)

You might have missed it, but go back again. Do you see it?

Jesus says, "… and when you have turned again…," implying that Peter would turn away, "… strengthen your brothers." This is incredible my friends. Not only does Jesus recognize that Peter would have a crisis of faith, but He ensures him that after Peter turns and then returns, he would still have a place in ministry.

His doubting would not deny him of his calling.

Jesus was telling Peter, "it's okay to wrestle, I still have a purpose and a plan waiting for you when you come back to me."

I need this, my friends. I need to know that God is okay with my tired and weary heart. I need to know that He is big enough to wrestle with and to be angry or upset with and that He will still have something for me to do after I am done. That none of my wonderings or wanderings will cancel it out.

This one truth is the greatest comfort I was gifted through our tragedy. The ability to roll around a little in my grief, in my debilitating pain, and say things that I would never truly mean in my right mind when everything is going right and my prayers are being answered the way I prayed for them to be answered. The knowing that His forgiveness would cover this too.

I hold on to this depiction of God in the middle of the night, Jacob walking away marked as one who will never be the same.

Jacob was victorious that day. Not because he got his way, not because he went toe to toe with God, but because he didn't stop until the light peaked back over the horizon. When the uncertainties settled and the warmth of the sunlight again hit his face, he was found with the same man that he had wrestled with all along. God. He never left him.

> I want to be like Jacob. I want to come rushing to meet with God like it depicts in Hebrews as "we do not have a high priest who is unable to sympathize with our weaknesses, but one who in every respect has been tempted as we are, yet without sin. Let us then with confidence draw near to the throne of grace, that we may receive mercy and find grace to help in time of need"
>
> (HEBREWS 4:15–16)

I need that grace to wage war in the night. I need to know that God is big enough to withstand the world-defining attacks on His character of being good and a miracle-worker. But more than anything, I need to plant my feet firm in the fight, not relenting until I am through the darkest parts knowing that I never retreated.

When we can commit to wrestling with God in the night, it changes us. We walk away different.

And we finally allow others to have their own struggles knowing that it isn't with us at all. In fact, I have found that the tension I was feeling all along was because I had placed myself in the spot of our Savior in the questioning and I needed to step back and let others wrestle too.

But you, beloved, building yourselves up in your most

holy faith and praying in the Holy Spirit, keep

yourselves in the love of God, waiting for the mercy of

our Lord Jesus Christ that leads to eternal life. And have

mercy on those who doubt. → *let them wrestle*

(JUDE 20-22)

pain is relentless, but so is God

Thursday, May 24, 2018: At this point in the week, John was so medicated that there was barely anything recognizable of him left as his body started swelling to what we joked was Andre the Giant status. He would be so impressed with how "swollen" he was considering his normal lanky posture. My brother had tried his entire life to gain weight. Stephanie and I joked about taking a picture to show to him later when he was awake again because by some miracle, some actual miracle, he survived the night.

After a handful of hours, Rich came through the doors. A nurse who had known John's wife Amanda for a few years had opened up a back conference room for us to stay in while they assessed the situation. Thursday morning we were left dazed and confused. He made it through the night, but what did that mean?

Was this just prolonging our pain and the inevitable? If it was going to be the end, then why would we be forced to suffer through each day with its ups and downs?

Mid-morning came and even more family gathered in the waiting room. My grandmothers both drove up from the Valley to say hello, and maybe their final goodbyes, while my father stayed hopeful that God would heal John's body. By this point I was a shell of a human without adequate sleep or nutrition and only wished to have an ounce of the faith that my father had.

After the doctors had done yet another test, asking all guests to vacate the room, we awaited a very important update on John's condition. When we heard the footsteps come to the door, all eyes looked up.

"John is still in very critical condition', he said, "but he is responding when people are in the room by blinking."

I looked at my husband with urgency and told him to go in with my dad. I knew that this would be the only chance we might get to ask that one very important question, and Rich knew it too. He went without any extra encouragement.

While they were in the room, the rest of us in the waiting room started to talk about John. We discussed what we would do in John's honor should he pass since my father protested our even mention of it, but with him away it was safe to do so. My sisters and mother agreed that crazy socks would have to be a part of the memorial service. It was John's signature look at the Defenders Court and how he was known by many colleagues. It is how we knew him as an incredibly smart young man with a super sarcastic side. It was decided. Then the room went quiet.

We were talking about it. Actually talking about it. How we would continue on without my brother. What we would do in his absence. It was almost too much to wrap my mind around, but at the same time, I knew in my gut that this would be the end. I knew it all along. Not because I had lost all faith that God could, but because in all of my praying and all of my pleading, I kept facing the resistance that God would.

In fact on our one night that John was doing well, the night we danced, I remember praying for God to raise my brother from his bed with the same power He raised Lazarus. I quoted the same passage of Scripture back to God as if He had somehow forgotten. I made a case for all of the reasons that He should make the same promise to me that He had to his friend Lazarus so that I had some shred of hope to hold onto. That John's situation "would not end in death" (John 11:4). But all I heard back was "yes, but his story *included* death."

I did not know what to make of it or what to pray for anymore. Was God going to heal him or wasn't He? Was He going to perform a miracle for my brother because we had already seen Him keep John alive through two very close calls that he should have never survived?

I did not understand.

Just then Rich walked back in. I wanted to run back to John's room knowing that I could finally switch out, and after the last night's events, it was incredibly important to be with him when he was still "in there" somewhere. For some reason I didn't jump up right away but lingered long enough to hear my husband attempt to make an announcement to the group.

"I asked John if he wanted to accept Jesus into His heart as his personal Lord and Savior," Rich started. It sounded very official. Almost too official.

I looked up at him from the couch where I had planted myself.

"He blinked once so I accepted that as a 'yes' and prayed over him."

My heart began racing. This is what we had been petitioning God for over the past decade since John decided that he did not believe anymore. I didn't know how to feel about it. Was he sure? Did John just blink to appease Rich or was it sincere? I wanted to believe that this was God's answer back to us. That He might have prolonged his death long enough to save his soul, but I wanted to be sure.

Then Rich continued, "I wanted to be sure" *you and me both, I thought*, "so I asked John after we had finished if he had prayed that prayer with us and he blinked again. He just kept blinking, maybe three or four times."

Soft crying made its way across the room. I couldn't make out if my own tears were because of the happiness over his decision, joy from my husband following the prompting of the Holy Spirit to ask... or sadness for what this might mean.

I tried to talk to myself, to make sense of it all. Whatever the case, John said the prayer. In his mind, where it mattered most, he said it.

I took my turn to sit by his bed and told John how thankful I was for his decision. I continued on with my stories of what Heaven would be like knowing that John might very well beat us all there.

Knowing how much he had struggled here on this earth, I wanted to remind him of the things we learned in Sunday school.

How Heaven was a place of no more crying or tears. How we would be perfectly at peace and full of joy where we were headed. How the Scriptures talk about God preparing a place just for us and that God loved him so much that He never gave up on him through it all.

Through the accidental hanging as a four-year old scared to fall off the side of the slide, tying a jump rope around his waist only to have slid down and have it thrust up around his neck. My mother who was about to get in the shower at the time felt the prompting of the Holy Spirit and needed to check on he and my younger sister "one more time" and found him nearly blue.

Through the motorcycle accident a few years prior when a woman pulled out in front of him causing his bike to be totaled and his fingers badly damaged. It could have been a million times worse.

Through the infection that led him to go to the emergency room time and time again only to be sent off with a pat on the head and some general antibiotics. The same infection that was later identified as the deadly bacteria C. diff creating a lot of panic and an emergency hazmat room to be set up in John's honor.

Through the suicide attempt just four months earlier when all hope was lost that his life would turn around. He took a power chord, tied it around his neck, and drifted off into the unknown only to be woken up again ten minutes later to his great surprise calling my sister in the middle of the night to say "I don't know why I woke up. I shouldn't be here."

Through the initial motorcycle accident that tore through his body, causing immediate paralysis and a whole slew of problems. Despite the back and head injuries, still giving us opportunities to communicate with him as he had his wits about him.

Through the awful experience we had ventured through the

night before with the certainty of death looming as his body could not keep the onslaught of infections under control.

It is like God let my brother cycle through two rounds of miracles—a hanging, motorcycle accident, infection followed by another hanging, motorcycle accident, and infection—to reach his stubborn self. He was relentless in second, third, fourth, fifth, and sixth chances because as much as I love my brother, God loves him more.

I finished off my time with him by playing some more of his music and then mixing in a few of my favorite worship songs. He was barely responsive at this point, so there would be no contest. I scrolled through my list until I landed on "Reckless Love" which has been surrounded by its own controversy, but in my brother's case, God's love felt a little reckless. Like He had gone off-roading through ditches and sand traps to fish my brother out of the wilderness. I wasn't sure before if I could sing that anything about Him was "careless" because God took great care in His concern of us, but this past week had changed my mind.

God was just as desperate for my brother as I was. As I sat by John's bed, tears still falling from my eyes, I told him that I loved him, but I wouldn't blame him if this world was too much for him to stay. At this point, it was too much for me too.

- - - - - - - - -

When I think of this moment, this one day during our horrible, no good, very bad week, I thank God.

Journeying this side of what I did not know then, but know now as John is no longer here, I cannot fathom what my grief would be like without it. I wish that the truth of his salvation was strong enough to pull me from my bed of sorrow most mornings when I am trying to convince myself to get up and conquer the world, but I am not there—yet.

What I am able to rejoice in without question is the obedience to the voice of the Holy Spirit that my husband displayed during such a desolate time. I am in awe that our God chose to visit Rich in a dream that would ultimately cause him to walk boldly into my brother's room and ask a question that had previously escaped me, "do you know Him?"

I like to think that all of my ramblings and mutterings over the years were seeds in the proverbial garden that decided now at the end to finally bloom through such stubborn soil, but the truth is that John could have made the decision unconsciously all along and we would have never known. The question was for us to know where he was. To know one way or the other where he stood and if we had any reason to have joy and hope.

The blink was for *us*.

When I first started this chapter, I had named it, "we have a part to play in the process" which I still believe with all of my heart. I still see God's hand and guidance woven in and out of the dark places. I still know that He has not left us and uses people in the process of it all. But this part of my brother's story, my story, declares more about God's love than our obedience, and I want to focus on that. So let's all agree that God still speaks and encourages us to take action amidst painful seasons if we choose to listen and obey so we can talk about the one thing that has wrecked me over and over again, ok?

We are Ninevah.

That is what God spoke to my heart while driving in the car talking with a friend about the conference that I had found myself in at the beginning of writing this story. *We are Ninevah.*

So many times while reading the book of Jonah in the Old Testament we talk about putting ourselves in the spot of the main character. We focus our attention on the wavering obedience of

Jonah, God's choosing only him to speak the message to the people, and how his emotions were a mess. I agree to all of these things. This is often what it looks like to be a fully devoted follower of Christ. We become uncertain, wishy-washy, knuckle-dragging, and grumblers when we are not in alignment with God's vision. When we do not see why a hateful, disruptful people need forgiveness or deserve grace and love.

That is why the Scriptures record that His "... thoughts are not your thoughts, neither are your ways My ways, declares the LORD. For as the heavens are higher than the earth, so are my ways higher than your ways and my thoughts than your thoughts" (Isaiah 55:8–9).

What we see is not what God is seeing.

My new favorite thing to ask in prayer is, "show me what you are seeing that I might be missing?" Because I am always missing something.

And that was the case with this book. What if we did not look at the story through the eyes of Jonah? What if we looked at the story through the even messier, more rebellious eyes of the lost people of Ninevah? The ones whom our God sent a prophet to, time after time even when Jonah chose to go the wrong way?

Now the word of the LORD came to Jonah the son of Amittai, saying, 'Arise, go to Nineveh, that great city, and call out against it, for their evil has come up before me.' But Jonah rose to flee to Tarshish from the presence of the LORD. He went down to Joppa and found a ship going to Tarshish. So he paid the fare and went down into it, to go with them to Tarshish, away from the presence of the LORD.

(JONAH 1:1–3)

What if God is actively doing whatever He can, through whatever means possible, to get our attention because He loves us and can't imagine an eternity without us.

Despite our mess?

Despite our rebellion and sin?

What if we are Ninevah???

Then the word of the LORD came to Jonah the second time, saying, 'Arise, go to Nineveh, that great city, and call out against it the message that I tell you.' So Jonah arose and went to Nineveh, according to the word of the LORD. Now Nineveh was an exceedingly great city, three days' journey in breadth. Jonah began to go into the city, going a day's journey. And he called out, 'Yet forty days, and Nineveh shall be overthrown!' And the people of Nineveh believed God. They called for a fast and put on sackcloth, from the greatest of them to the least of them.

(JONAH 3:1–5)

I don't know if this grips you the way that it grips me, but I can't get over it.

The Scriptures say that "For while we were still weak, at the right time Christ died for the ungodly. For one will scarcely die for a righteous person—though perhaps for a good person one would dare even to die— but God shows his love for us in that while we were still sinners, Christ died for us" (Romans 5:6–8).

While we were running.

While we were disobedient.

While we doubted.

While we mocked and argued and denied Him.

While we were our most unlovable, God loved us in the most unrelenting of ways.

This is the story of humanity and its reconciliation, our story.

If you feel like you have been caught in the mud, like you are a far way off from God, I am praying that you can understand this. That you are never "too much" or "too far gone" for Him.

He loves you. He always has. He always will. Nothing (no sin or shame or distance or rejection) can separate us from His love (see Romans 8:35–39). And when we turn from our sin and ask forgiveness, He never turns us away. In fact, our salvation mimics that of Ninevah: *not* getting what we rightly deserve:

When God saw what they did, how they turned from their evil way, God relented of the disaster that he had said he would do to them, and he did not do it. (Jonah 3:10)

If you are feeling the urge to ask Jesus to come into your life as your personal Lord and Savior, making Heaven your home in eternity, or to rededicate your life because you feel like you have drifted into your own wilderness far from Him, then I would be honored to pause my brother's story to give you the same opportunity that was gifted to John. To say yes.

All that the Word requires you must do is "declare with your mouth, 'Jesus is Lord,' and believe in your heart that God raised him from the dead, you will be saved" (Romans 10:9). This guarantees your name is on the invite list. This confirms that when you journey from this life into the next, Heaven is your home.

And if you get there before I do, please give John a hug for me, and let him know that you are there because God saw through time and space to reach you through his story.

If you want to do that today, simply pray this prayer:

Jesus, I believe that You came to this earth more than two-thousand years ago to make the way for your most cherished creation—humanity—to find their way back to You. Thank you for living in such a way that I have a perfect example to follow. Thank you for dying for my sins that were too much for me to atone for so that I can hold on to hope for my future. And thank you for rising again after the third day defeating death, Hell, and the grave so that I can spend an eternity with you. Please, come into my life and be the Savior and Redeemer of my soul. Amen.

If we confess our sins, he is faithful and just

and will <u>forgive</u> us our sins and purify us

from all unrighteousness.

all of it.
He forgives
all of it

(1 JOHN 1:9)

You are not too far gone, too broken, too dirty,
too sinful, too anything, for God to love you and
give you a fresh start

focus on God, not a good outcome

Friday, May 25, 2018: We were closing in on John being in the hospital for an entire week. Our bodies were exhausted and malnourished and full of insecurities with how God would answer our prayers. Would we get our miracle so that John's life could be the embodiment of the power of God, or would his story include death like God had slowly been prompting me?

My mind shifted to a friend who had just lost her sister the month before, and I stepped out to text her to find some encouragement.

I asked her how she did it.

How she lived without her sister because I just didn't know how I was going to do it. And even beyond that, how she ventured the great unknown until futures where certain and things were final. In all of the waiting and wishing and praying until there were answers.

Her response, "You have hope. You have hope until you don't have hope. But until then, you have hope."

Now of course her words were much more extensive and beautiful and carried more relief than I can put into words almost nine months later, but that one thought stuck in my head. Having hope until there is no hope. Until the very last moment.

I would love to say that I walked around the hospital calling Heaven down, but with every turn it was more and more bleak. "It's not a matter of 'if' but 'when'," they would tell us. So we waited for his death.

One of the last times that I was alone with my brother, I sat beside him as the doctors had been able to rotate him a full 180 degrees to let the mucus formed from the infection drain from his body. I watched as it hung from his nose and joked with the nurse that he was paid the big bucks to wipe it. Truth be told, I would have wiped it if he had handed me the tissue. I would have done anything for my brother.

John had stopped responding as his body slowly shut down more and more. He had five organ systems in failure, but taking him off of the strong medications that he was on to keep his heart and lungs going would cause certain death, even if it meant prolonged suffering. It was a lose–lose situation.

By this time Brad had reluctantly left for Southern California as his brother was getting married that weekend. He didn't want to leave us, or leave John, but there was nothing that any of us could do. My brother was going downhill fast.

I didn't have any more words to say, so I put my phone near his ears and continued to play his favorite band. This time I had found Wi-Fi and had downloaded the entire album so we wouldn't be stuck with just one song. I don't know if he could feel or sense my sitting there staring at him, but I so badly wanted to hear him make one more joke. Or for him to be awake enough for me to tell him things that I had never been brave enough to say before.

Things like how I had blamed myself for his turning away from God since I jumped into a life of ministry becoming his first youth pastor neglecting my first role as a sister in the process. How I so badly wanted to be loved and accepted by many that the most important people in my life got the short end of the stick time and time again. How I should have made more time to visit or not get so upset with him when he would be ornery around the boys, thinking that he would sway them to be just as pessimistic or ornery too. How I would have quit my job and lived in Northern California until he was able to get completely settled on his own in a heartbeat ignoring every other responsibility if he decided to fight. Because I so desperately wanted him to fight.

But mostly, how I was struggling to reconcile professing faith but possessing none when the rubber met the road. How my thoughts were continually justifying each new report about his condition and my prayers for a painless exit from this life into the other.

I didn't say these things because I didn't want him to think that he broke me especially so soon after blinking through the sinner's prayer. I wanted to be strong, for him, and for everyone else watching. No matter the amount of responses we received via social media and GoFundMe when sharing John's updates, the feeling of utter loneliness and complete draining of strength never left.

I wanted to share a good story with everyone, but I knew it wasn't going to be that. John was going to die, and that was the story that I would have to write.

I walked back into the waiting room for another person to take their shift, repeating the words of my friend in my head, "You have hope. You have hope until you don't have hope. But until then, you have hope."

- - - - - - - -

I wish that I could say that I executed this charge for carrying hope with great courage—but the truth is that I didn't. This lesson, the one we share together in this chapter, was the most delayed of all.

Six months after my brother's funeral, I had found my way back to Northern California which has always been a place of familiarity and safety being our home for over fifteen years, but it had somehow lost its luster for me. My life had been dulled by the glaring absence of my brother, and there was no going back to normal or popping in for spontaneous visits anymore. Everything would now need to be planned to a "t" accounting for any emotional sustaining measures needed to "get through" being "there" again. Grief took this from me too; it just kept taking it seemed.

That Sunday morning was no different. I sat in the back of the church that I had grown up in, that I met Jesus in, that I went to bible college in, that I met my husband in, that I got married in, that we pastored in… and that we said our goodbyes to my brother in. It was my first time back since that day, and while I still had thousands of memories that I could pull on to put a smile on my face, the only one that I wanted to forget was the one that wouldn't leave me.

Seeing his face on the screen and standing in front of friends and family telling myself to be strong and say something nice.

So on this, the first time back, I was, in fact, sullen.

I thought about hiding it, and I thought about putting on the happy face because it is what people want to see, maybe even expect to see, but I was hurting and I let myself be free from faking, for even if just this moment. After all, I was in God's house and He already knew the condition of my heart.

The pastor's wife spotted me at the end of service and, upon finding my puffy red eyes that had shifted somewhere toward the ground, simply said, "Oh Vanessa, you've lost your joy." And then she gave me a hug and prayed over me and said words that I wish I could remember, but she was right and my sadness had blocked them out. My sadness had blocked a lot out. But I could tell you that her hug and genuine care for my heart made me want to find my way back again. To find the joy that I had lost.

So, per the usual lately, I forgot about the exchange of words until a few weeks later when I needed to create a Christmas card. This one would be for our family just after Thanksgiving, so I wanted it to be full of encouragement knowing what lies ahead. If anything, just for me. That's when that word popped up again among the slew of pre-formatted Christmas greetings, "joy."

Being a pastor, I like to add a verse to make it the most effective as the Word never returns void, so I pulled out my bible and found these words to add to our signature at the bottom: "May the God of hope fill you with all joy and peace...," taken from Romans 15:13 which continues to say, "... in believing, so that by the power of the Holy Spirit you may abound in hope."

It turns out that the joy that I had been missing was more attached to the hope that I had lost all along.

A hope for my brother to be healed, a hope for his life to be restored, and a hope for his miracle testimony to change lives. The hope I lost when God decided instead to use his accident to reach his soul for an eternity and let him enter the gates of Heaven. And while it was truly glorious, it was also excruciating and nothing at all what I was *hoping* for.

Hope is a funny thing. The definition found in the Merriam-Webster Dictionary is "to desire with expectation of obtainment or fulfillment, to expect with confidence: trust." And then there is this funny notation at the end of it that says, "To hope without any basis for expecting fulfillment" (Merriam-Webster n.d.).

I recognized that kind of hope. I saw it in Abraham when Paul was giving an account for his journey to receiving the promise he was given. It says in Romans 4:18 that "*in* hope he believed *against* hope, that he should become the father of many nations, as he had been told...." I read that first part a few more times to let it sink in.

In hope he believed *against* hope.

How? How can you do this? How can you be "in" something and "against" it at the same time? That is physically impossible, and I was right. It is impossible to be in and against something at the same time—unless... well, unless that one hope was actually two opposing hopes. If it in fact was the battle between what we could plausibly put our confidence and trust in based on outcomes and experience and who we could put our trust in based on our faith.

I love the way the Matthew Henry commentary puts it; it says of this passage:

There was a hope against [Abraham], a natural hope. All the arguments of sense, and reason, and experience, which in such cases usually beget and support hope, were against him; no second causes smiled upon him, nor in the least favoured his hope. But, against all those inducements to the contrary, he believed; for he had a hope for him: He believed in hope, which arose, as his faith did, from the consideration of God's all-sufficiency. That he might become the father of many nations. (Henry 1706)

What am I asking of myself then? That I throw years of sibling bond away and disregard an entire life's existence and subsequent giant hole that was left as if some euphoric world existed where it didn't bring an insurmountable amount of pain? To "buck up little buckaroo" and "fake it till you make it" as if any months or years of passing will erase the fact that there is an empty chair where someone we loved dearly sat? Can someone really do this?

I propose instead that I might have mixed up my hopes to which, if I continued in this way, would only lead to a life full of sorrow and depression and feelings of defeat. (Notice that I did not say sadness as that is a natural emotional reaction to loss and is different from committing yourself to a life of sadness. It's not the same.)

Scripture instructs us to fight against hope, in hope.

Against the hope found in our circumstances, in the hope of a loving God. Not against the hope of our loving God, in the hope of our circumstances.

Because, friends, sometimes the results of our circumstances—found in momentary pauses of reflection to assess where you are in your story and in your journey—will cause you to believe that your hope is lost. As if this is where it ended and there was nothing else.

While reading a new book from one of my favorite authors Lysa TerKeurst (TerKeurst 2018), I was reminded of this truth. That hope is not meant to be placed in answered prayers or outcomes. Because we have a whole list of those. We are the best at writing down exactly what God *should* do and how He should do it. I think that Peter is a great example of this. Peter is a great example of a lot of things, but particularly this one idea.

And in the fourth watch of the night he came to them, walking on the sea. But when the disciples saw him walking on the sea, they were terrified, and said, 'It is a ghost!' and they cried out in fear. But immediately Jesus spoke to them, saying, 'Take heart; it is I. Do not be afraid.' And Peter

answered him, 'Lord, if it is you, command me to come to
you on the water.' He said, 'Come.' So Peter got out of the
boat and walked on the water and came to Jesus. But when
he saw the wind, he was afraid, and beginning to sink he
cried out, 'Lord, save me.' Jesus immediately reached out
his hand and took hold of him, saying to him, 'O you of little
faith, why did you doubt?' And when they got into the boat,
the wind ceased. And those in the boat worshiped him, saying, 'Truly you are the Son of God.'

(MATTHEW 14:25–33)

When we read the account, we may not see right away that
Peter has a false sense of hope. He put his trust in the "walking on
water," and when circumstances declared to him that it was too difficult, it says that Peter "saw the wind" and "was afraid." Why did
he shift his eyes? Why did he stop looking at Jesus? Jesus was still
standing on the waves despite the storm. What changed? Could it
be that Peter puts his hope in an idea that Jesus would calm the
storm like he had time and time again before he stepped out of
the boat?

Because friends, Jesus wasn't calming this storm. He was calling Peter to walk on the water *despite* the storm. I wondered if
this is where I had allowed myself to be. Was my hope, my joy,
bound to John living? In His making my situation calm and "ok"
ad "good"? Bound to God answering my prayers the way I wanted
them answered, or was it steadfast in God Himself?

I love that Paul writes in Hebrews 12:2: "Looking to Jesus, the
founder and perfecter of our faith...." It does not say, looking to
our faith. Our faith for what He will do. Our faith for how He will do
it. No, we are to look to Jesus and Him alone.

This does not mean that we are to give up asking God to go to
work in our lives. Friend, I have a whole list of things I am believing
in faith for. But my hope is not wrapped up in those things. My

hope is in the God in whom I am asking. So ask the hard questions, and tell Him what is concerning you and how you are believing for Him to come through. But please don't walk away when it doesn't come to fruition how you imagined. The ending is never how we completely imagine it because of the idea we talked about in the last chapter—God sees things that we don't. Which is also something we talk about in the next chapter. Because it really affects everything. Literally everything.

So much of our faith and hope have the potential to be damaged due to our seeing things differently. But don't be discouraged. Even Abraham's story didn't originally turn out like he had wanted (you know, with the maidservant and Ishmael and all), but still God's purpose was fulfilled. Because it isn't the end yet. Even when we think things are final and there is no more hope, even then it is still not the end.

When we plant our feet and put our hope in a God, our God, who is patient and kind and steadfast, we can weather any obstacle with an assurance in knowing that just as passionately as He sent His Son to this earth to take our punishment in His place—He stands in the middle of the storm to help you walk through the midst of it. Stay focused and watch the horizon.

He is coming for you. Don't lose focus.

fix your focus. Vanessa

Looking to Jesus, the founder and perfecter of our faith,

who for the joy that was set before Him endured the

WE

were
the
joy

cross, despising the shame, and is seated at the right

hand of the throne of God.

(HEBREWS 12:2)

CHAPTER NINE

God's plan sometimes includes pain

Saturday, May 26, 2018: One week after my brother's accident and we were grasping at straws. Looking at the dialysis machine that was started earlier that morning just confirmed our worst fears as his blood was too thick to even funnel in and out of the machine without clotting. The newest doctor on my brother's case sat the family down inside of the conference room where we had stayed that one dreadful night when things were too close to death for our comfort.

He told the family that we needed to choose how John would die. He didn't word it like that, but it is exactly what he meant.

Would it be by the medication that was keeping his heart going that was also causing organ failure, or would we let him go by removing care and allowing his body to pass away on its own terms?

We knew what John wanted. He had told us to "junk him" at one point in the whole ordeal because he hated the idea of being on machines and he knew his injuries were extensive. Not to mention the idea of being paralyzed was not an easy pill to swallow for someone with a history of depression and a suicide attempt. The decision was an easy one. (*I say easy in the sense that it came to us quickly, but the actual deed of expressing this thought out loud was by all means the same as an act of treason to everything I hold dear. My family. The sanctity of life. The idea of fighting to live. Everything. But it was right nonetheless.*)

At 8:00 pm, while my mother's side of the family all gathered in Chino Hills, CA, to celebrate with my cousin and his new bride on a day that should have been the happiest for everyone involved, my immediate family gathered around John's bedside as each medication was slowly reduced, one by one.

It was gut-wrenchingly painful and peaceful all at once. I held onto his swollen arm and kissed it over and over, hoping that he would feel the warmth of it as he made this one last journey.

My mother asked if we could play his favorite band to fill the void (and mask the beeping of the many machines that still littered the silence in the room). I pulled it out and mom placed it on his shoulder. The techno music and upbeat tones contrasted the cold that had settled, but this moment was for him, not for us, so we allowed it.

This day, what would happen in this room would mark to us for the rest of our lives.

We watched his chest rise and fall as the breathing machine contrasted and expanded. Up, down, up, down. Somewhere in the middle of the ups and downs, John had passed. They hadn't even finished weaning him off of all of the medication before his body decided to succumb to death.

It was 8:40 pm.

We cried. Heavy life-altering tears. My father lifted a clenched fist that I just knew was going to be put through the wall, which he might have initially intended before my mom called out to him. He instead used his fist to help him lean against the side of the room in an effort to keep him upright as he sobbed unrelenting tears. This final vision was not what he was hoping for at all. But it was final still.

My mother reached over to take the phone from my brother's shoulder where it had been placed as it was still playing John's songs. She placed it back in my hands, and I felt God urge me to play just one more thing. Not from his playlist but from my own.

"Can I play one last song?" I asked the group.

Everyone nodded in agreement. I scrolled down to a song that had given me hope in a hopeless time after my youth pastor had passed away a few years prior. I hit play and placed it on his abdomen.

This song would be for us... but I knew he would have approved of it, too.

The words rang more true now than ever before as we listened to the words speak of the very moment we leave this earth and enter the next. (*If you haven't heard the song, "Tears of Joy" by Phil Wickham, I encourage you to look it up and let it speak to your soul like it spoke to ours that night.*) It was exactly what we needed as we endured exactly what we wished we never would.

The lyrics captured my heart and a steadfast peace like never before came flooding in. This was the worst day, the worst moment, the worst pain I have ever experienced, and yet, I was gifted the ability to rejoice because God let him live over and over—until a blink changed his eternity causing him to live forevermore.

We grabbed hands one last time as a family and prayed one last prayer. This time asking for God to welcome our brother home and to give us strength, abandoning our previous pleas to keep him here with us.

What a profound, stupid prayer, I thought. It was both to me.

We didn't want to taint the happy memories of a family wedding with the announcement of John's death, so we resolved to tell the family in the morning, reaching out to only a select few family members that had been checking in for updates.

We gathered our items that had now overtaken the waiting room that we had claimed as our own and walked out of the hospital for the last time.

I whispered, "My brother is dead," just to hear myself say it. It sounded like a lie but walking to our cars, just the five of us now, screamed back to me how true it was.

While crawling into bed that night, I started checking previous well wishes from family and friends online and stumbled upon a post from a previous family member who had divorced from the family during our childhood years. The words that were written spoke of John being in God's presence now and I gasped. I messaged her as fast as I could to ask her to take it down, wondering how in the world she had found out and praying that no one had seen it as we weren't yet ready to share.

I sent the message and then I sat up in my bed waiting for her reply. Praying to God most of all that my mother hadn't stumbled upon it. The woman responded back in utter confusion. I told her what happened, that John had died and that we are trying to hold off letting people know until the morning. I ended my message by sternly urging her to, "please take your post down."

She had no idea.

She apologized profusely and then spoke about a vision she had while praying for our family, specifically my brother, and how God had shown her that His light was all around John. How God was with him and everything would be ok.

I didn't like it. I was mad. Mainly because I wanted to have John with us, and as I cried myself to sleep, my frustrations grew. It wasn't fair. I let myself get really angry for a few minutes before I allowed that vision of John being whole and in the presence of the God I had always known as loving and kind to really sink in. John had made it home. After years of begging with the Lord to send someone, He used this accident and my husband to usher him into Heaven. And now we would have the opportunity to see him again. I forced myself to focus on that. *We would see him again.*

After the first full night of uninterrupted sleep I had gotten in over a week, I woke up with that image of John standing before God in my mind. It didn't provoke anger in me anymore. Instead I cried tears of joy for the reconciliation that my brother was experiencing. Oh how I longed to join him at the feet of His throne, singing with the angels. That euphoric feeling lasted only a few minutes, and then it was gone.

What followed next was a lot of crying in the middle of stores while picking out socks to wear to my brother's funeral, numbingly flipping through scrapbooks that would be filled with memories with family and friends, and long showers that could never wash away the debilitating sorrow I was now experiencing.

Grief. It's the worst.

- - - - - - - -

We moved from one hotel to another, and I fought the desire to get out and do something with staying in and sleeping all day. There was no in-between, and nothing felt safe and secure anymore.

That Wednesday our family came together for our first family adventure without my brother as we entered the same tattoo parlor that John had frequented months prior to talk to the owner about the sleeve he wanted him to design and buy bigger gauges for his ears. I watched as one by one each of us hopped onto the chair to be inked and jokingly told my parents, "maybe the next family trip we can just go to Disneyland" as our first family get-to-gether was quite out of the ordinary. At least for us it was. I may or may not have had a few tattoos already (ok a whole arm's worth), and my older sister had quite a few herself, but Bethany and my parents had never jumped on that bandwagon.

Their marking their bodies with a bent bow being shot into heaven to represent my brother's ascent was a vision I will not soon forget.

Just when I thought that I could regroup and figure out this whole living thing again, my knees were swept from under me as the day before John's funeral I stumbled upon the social media announcement of a close mentor's passing. One we would find out later was self-inflicted.

Standing in the hotel room reading words about someone's demise after walking through almost two weeks of coming to terms with death in the most personally invasive of ways felt monstrous. It was like someone had stolen the air from my lungs again, and I struggled to process what I was reading. I called my husband seeing as we had worked with this man for three years while living in Stockton, CA, Rich continuing to work a few hours each week remotely, and he being so close to him I was unsure if he had heard yet. He had.

This man had introduced me to Jesus as a fifteen-year-old broken girl and had been the catalyst for me trading in my hopelessness for my faith in a God who would never let us down. This was that man.

God why??? Why this? Why now? If he couldn't make it, how was I supposed to?

Rich's voice was shaking as he answered the phone. He confirmed what I had just read. He even added that he had just gotten off of the phone with a close personal friend who had been at the house with the family all morning.

This man, this hero, had so impacted our family that there was nothing that anyone could do to prepare us for this. Especially after John's passing. And my brother-in-law before that. It felt like a cruel joke. How was my husband supposed to be strong for us now? How was he supposed to give me room and grace to grieve when he himself was in immeasurable pain?

Everything was upside down and not how I imagined God turning things around for our good as it is promised in Scripture.

I was holding onto those words about "[knowing] for those who love God all things work together for good, for those who are called according to His purpose" (Romans 8:28). I was waiting for it. Expecting it. I didn't need it to happen right away, but how does one go about preaching God's sovereign plan through suffering when God feels distant and silent and allows tragedy to happen upon tragedy?

I knew that I would trust Him beyond my feelings, no matter how hard and unfathomable my circumstances might get, but how were the many watching supposed to manage with their already mounting concerns about God's goodness?

Was God not concerned with how hard He was making it

for others to come to know Him through their already darkened lenses?

What about my children? How was I supposed to show them that God could be trusted when so many of our requests had gone unanswered in the way that we were asking for them to be answered? Was God still in the miracle business, or had we gone so far from His covering that we had been left to suffer the consequences on our own?

I knew God was here, somewhere, but I couldn't see Him.

I am not sure if you have ever felt this way, struggling to make sense of your circumstances in a way that makes God out to be good and still in control, but for me it is a regular occurrence.

Honestly, I feel like my life lately has been the actual representation of the meme with the captain of the Titanic pictured at the helm of the sinking ship with the words overhead that read "This is fine. Everything is fine." I speak fluent memes, and this one is saved to my phone for occasions such as these when I go into survival mode replacing actual thoughts with witty sarcasm instead. It is a real thing. Humor helps me. It's biblical (see Proverbs 17:22).

There has not been one time throughout our journey that we haven't been able to laugh, even if it meant shoving all of our feelings aside to do so. I have now deemed myself a professional at cracking a joke in the middle of a teary meltdown. Because I need things to be funny as much as I need them to make sense. And guess what I have found in the process? It is easier to find humor than the meaning for pain.

Jesus is not immune from this struggle.

We have talked a lot before of His struggle in the garden. Sweating actual blood and pleading with God to find another way for our salvation. But this was the way. The only way. So instead of waiting on an explanation from His Father, at least one written for us to read, Jesus allows Himself to be betrayed, arrested, falsely accused, sentenced to die, beaten, and hung on a cross.

This is where I have found my greatest comfort. In Jesus' words while He was suffering excruciating pain:

And when the sixth hour had come, there was darkness over the whole land until the ninth hour. And at the ninth hour Jesus cried with a loud voice, 'Eloi, Eloi, lema sabach-thani?' which means, 'My God, my God, why have you forsaken me?' And some of the bystanders hearing it said, 'Behold, he is calling Elijah.' And someone ran and filled a sponge with sour wine, put it on a reed and gave it to him to drink, saying, 'Wait, let us see whether Elijah will come to take him down.' And Jesus uttered a loud cry and breathed his last.

(MARK 15:33–37)

First of all (said with all of the sass that I possess in my bones, which is a lot), I would have words for these people who are *watching* the entire thing unfold and decide for themselves what God should be doing to prove Himself or His Son. They are the physical representation of the phrase "if you light a fire, people will come to watch it burn." They were there for the show.

Lord, give me strength for these people.

Which of course brings me to the second thing. The question I now find myself asking. Have my actions been more reflective of Jesus or the onlookers in this story? And what I mean by that is, have I allowed myself to talk to God about my frustrations or to everyone else while I seek to make sense of it all? Have I rested in His plan or made suggestions about how He could be actively redeeming it? If I were to be honest with myself, it was probably more the latter than the former.

In this story, Jesus, being our perfect example, shows how we trudge through the really difficult parts of life. With validating our feelings and realities… to God.

I cannot describe how much I love that Jesus is not on the cross saying "this is fine. Everything is fine." Because it wasn't. This was not fine. No, instead Jesus asks why God has to remove His presence from Him and loudly cries. I need to repeat that even if just for myself. *Jesus asks why God has to remove His presence from Him and loudly cries.*

This is the acceptable response to pain, which is a natural part of life and God's plan. If it weren't so, then there would have never been a crucifixion much less a beheading of John the Baptist, martyr of most of the disciples, or imprisonment of Paul and Silas, not to mention all of the other times Paul was imprisoned or put on house arrest.

All of these examples of human suffering were included in God's plan, but don't misunderstand me—God did not plan them.

This is the confusing portion for many as we raise our voices and scream at the Heavens asking God to stop what He never started. God didn't do this. If you hear nothing else, please try to grasp this one thing, that God didn't do this. He just allowed it.

In the salvation story of humanity, God allowed what He knew would be persecution and suffering to occur so that, through it, anyone who would call on His name would and now could be saved. God didn't cause the pain but He gave it a purpose.

I wish I could say that after a lot of prayers and cry sessions, I obediently (and willingly) walked through trials, but I have more often than not been the person on the sidelines that keeps telling God what He should do to make sense of it all.

I see Your Son is dying here, God; maybe You should send someone to help. Maybe that Elijah fellow. That would really prove your existence and goodness to all of these here onlookers. Mainly me. It would prove it to me.

I don't believe myself to mock God or question His existence, but I have been known a time or two to try and figure out what He is doing or should be doing well before I can see the picture fully.

I also would love to think that God would let me in on what He is doing, but truth be told I am sometimes the last to know. Maybe God understands that I would muck it up so I have to wait with everyone else before the meaning He is creating from my mess becomes clear?

Fortunately for the crowd that had gathered to see Jesus crucified, they wouldn't have to wait too long. The Scriptures continue to say:

> And the curtain of the temple was torn in two, from top to bottom. And when the centurion, who stood facing him, saw that in this way he breathed his last, he said, 'Truly this man was the Son of God!'
>
> (MARK 15:38–39)

Jesus was confirmed as the Son of God not by His being rescued, but by His death. Let that sink in.

I would think that God showing up in miraculous ways would be more powerful at drawing lost people to redemption than any terrible situation, but God, knowing the hearts and minds of people, knew that Jesus *had* to die. That it was the only way.

And three days later after defeating death, Hell, and the grave, Jesus rose again so that we can spend our eternities with a loving God who had been until that moment separated, moment by moment dependent upon the follow-through of a repentant sacrifice. Now we just need to say a repentant prayer and accept the sacrifice already made for us.

God made the pain into a two for one. Confirming His Son's identity and our inheritance through Jesus' pain.

When I think back on the day that my brother died, I cannot say that I was sure of God's presence or that through it someone came to agree that He exists. It was awful and heartbreaking and the opposite of what we were believing for. But despite all of that, what I do believe all this time later is that God knew what it would take to get my brother into Heaven. And while He doesn't cause pain, God knows how to lean into it to pull the most He can from the situation so that none of it goes to waste.

He leans into pain.

So much of my life has been spent trying to escape pain that I have missed the beauty of what can be gifted back to us when we lean into it.

And, if for nothing else, my brother is now walking on streets of gold and singing with the angels. His death was not for naught.

Beyond that, there are hundreds of people who have encountered our family both in America and overseas who have gained comfort and strength from John's story. His death was not for naught.

And finally, I am a different person. In the best (but sometimes what feels as the worst) way. I care more deeply, love more expressively, and wait more intentionally than ever before. I have a newfound strength that was never there and a hope that Heaven is waiting for me when my time is done. And now my brother is waiting for me when my time is done. His death was not for naught.

The plan that God saw from the beginning of time for John's life included pain, but He saw it fit to not rescue him from it. And I am so glad He didn't.

We can trust Him. With the good things of life and with the pain.

I will conclude this one lesson with one of my favorite quotes I have ever read about God's plan and our suffering. It is by Charles Swindoll who once said:

His plan includes all promotions and demotions. His plan can mean both adversity and prosperity, tragedy and calamity, ecstasy and joy. It envelops illness as much as health, perilous times as much as comfort, safety, prosperity and ease. His plan is at work when we cannot imagine why, because it is so unpleasant, as much as when the reason is clear and pleasant. His sovereignty, though it is inscrutable, has dominion over all handicaps, all heartaches, all helpless moments. It is at work through all disappointments, broken dreams, and lingering difficulties. And even when we cannot fully fathom why, he knows. Even when we cannot explain the reasons, He understands. And when we cannot see the end, He is there nodding, 'Yes, that is my plan.' (Swindoll 2001) *this is not a suggestion*

(Trust) in the LORD with all your heart, and <u>do not</u> lean

on your own understanding. In all your ways

acknowledge him, and he will make straight your paths.

(PROVERBS 3:5-6)

Trust that God is
at work in every situation.
He is going ahead of you
and making – forcing –
the crooked paths. straight

strong isn't what we think it is

Saturday, June 2, 2018: The day of my brother's funeral was nearing, and despite all of the ways I had attempted to reprieve for self-care, coffee with a friend and spending six hours in a salon just to get my hair chopped off and colored, I was not prepared.

The girls decided to sneak away together for a little girl time before seeing All. The. People. at John's service. A few weeks prior, my sisters, mother, and I had all gotten our nails done for Bethany's wedding, so being back in a nail salon all together so soon felt wrong. There was nothing to celebrate. Nothing to get dolled up for. Nothing to laugh about as we picked out our polish colors and took our places on the chairs to wait for our names to be called.

There were tears, somber looks of defeat, and forced smiles of assurance from across the room as we looked to each other for strength.

Even if no one else knew what we had just walked through, we knew. But of course I am not the only over-sharer in my family, so by the end of our time everyone knew. It was hard not to tell people at this point. It felt like our entire world had stopped and shifted, and yet for everyone else nothing had changed at all.

The world carried on as business as usual and that was a hard pill to swallow. The usual. The normal. Because our new normal was now smacking us in the face begging to be accepted, and we wanted none of it. So we talked about John. About our journey. In some odd way, it allowed us to relive the part of our lives where he was still a part of it. It was sad and awful but our new realities were worse. The use of past tense verbs to describe a person you love will always be worse.

When we woke up the morning of the funeral, I had yet to know what I wanted to say about my brother. I could not grasp what few words could encapsulate an entire life. Or how, for that matter, I would be able to get through it without a complete mental breakdown.

I turned the worship music on, put on my black dress, and hesitantly tugged and pulled at every piece of hair in the mirror that seemed out of place until I realized that I wasn't trying to change anything about my appearance at all. I was trying to figure out how we got here. How we could manage to make sense of the horror we were facing. A funeral for an otherwise mostly healthy twenty-seven-year-old man that left the house one fateful day to feel the sun on his skin and the wind in his face. Riding made him feel like he was one with nature. It made him feel free. I tried to remind myself that where he was he was free indeed, but nothing could cover the gaping hole that now existed in our family.

I knew that I needed to say something about him when it was our turn to share, the three sisters, so I grabbed a brightly colored index card and scribbled a few things down.

"Glitter jellies and skirts.
Summer school in the playhouse.
Funny cards at Walmart."

Those were the things that reminded me of my brother. I tucked the neon pink card into the pocket of my dress and piled into the car headed to the church to say our final farewell.

An incredible local business had reached out to offer a pre-service lunch for our entire family (which was not small), so we shuffled into the room where the food would be delivered and relatives who had spent the morning driving in had started to gather. As much as everything had solidified our love and need for family, it also made gathering together very difficult because all that invaded my mind was the thought that "John should be here." Everyone was here, except him. He should be here.

I walked around the room for a few minutes until retreating to the sanctuary where the actual service would be held. It was empty. Just God and me. Well God, me, and the giant picture of my brother that encompassed the large screens mounted in the front of the room. I stared at them. Thinking that the picture selected was not the one my mother would have wanted. Then of course I fell apart in the back of the church because I was staring at my brother's picture. My brother. The only one I had.

I texted my husband with the picture that my mother would have wanted and let him take care of getting it handled. He was really good at that. And then I composed myself to appear strong, returning to the room full of our family who might not have even noticed my disappearance with all of the hustle and bustle.

There was only one thing that I had wanted from that room. To see my cousin's new wife. To say congratulations, of course, but also because they had been at Bethany's wedding where John had spontaneously taken the mic to make a toast to the new couple. He wasn't slated to, but since Stephanie and I had already shared our own well wishes and hilarious memories, John wanted a crack at it, too. Bethany and John were inseparable as children, so we knew that he would have a plethora of embarrassing stories to share which would be the icing on the cake. And it was just as we hoped it would be.

John had everyone in stitches. And then he ended it with the sincerest of compliments to the youngest Benbow. Despite his own feelings of marriage as his had turned out to have failed, he doted on the new couple and wished them their happily ever after. It was beautiful. It was also the only thing my sisters and I wanted after his passing. This one thing to remember him by. Which is why I was hunting for my cousin's new wife who had been spotted that evening with a video recorder in her hands.

I scoured the room and found the newlyweds in the food line. Without a second thought, I walked right up to them giving them a short but genuine congratulations followed by a quick inquiry to if she might have caught the speech in her tape. My stomach turned in knots for the brief milliseconds between my question and her answer. I didn't want to think of what it would be like to let go of any hope to hear his voice in such a loving way talking about his family. Stephanie, Bethany, and I were desperate to have those words captured to share not just with each other but with our children who would soon forget more and more of him as each year passed.

"Yes. I got it!" She exclaimed.

I thanked them repeatedly and then b-lined for my sisters who were a little further back in line.

"Nancy got it!" I shrieked.

"Got what?" There was some confusion as to what I was actually referring to, which of course was understandable as I tried to hold my composure.

"John's speech at the wedding. She got it on film" (*insert all the tears from three very weary sisters who were trying their best to hold it together*).

We cried and hugged and thanked God. It was the best gift and the only thing we were wanting since his passing. To have this one speech.

With the knowledge that a part of my brother's memory was preserved, we took our seats in the church as the service was starting, awaiting our turns to take the stage. We were going to do it together.

I had been in that church so many times, even being on the stage a handful of times, but never like this. I reached into my pocket to find that wrinkled card so I wouldn't forget what I was going to say and waited for Bethany to finish to cue when I would speak.

Don't cry, Vanessa. I told myself. Be strong, I said.

Bethany got a few words in before she started to uncontrollably sob on the stage. For whatever reason I thought it appropriate to mutter under my breath, "don't be a weeny," as a terrible form of encouragement meant to help her get through the rest of what she wanted to say. I don't know why I did this. But I did. I still kick myself for that one.

When my turn came, I spoke of the relationship that I had with my brother. Dressing him up in glitter jellies, large shirts that fit him like dresses, and a skirt over his head to cast him as whatever part we imagined that day in our numerous plays we thought up for our mother. I spoke of how when my younger siblings were on summer break I would hold them hostage in the playhouse that our father built to do a makeshift summer school with real homework and schoolbooks and everything. And then I finished my trip down memory lane with something my brother and I shared—just him and me.

Whenever we would find ourselves in stressful situations, John and I would jump into my car and go to our local Walmart to read the funny cards. It was our thing. We got such a kick out of reading birthday inscriptions that referenced bodily functions, extreme old age, or anything found in the humor section with a dog on the cover.

We Benbows are no quiet people, and I assure you that most of the store could hear us cackling our way down the aisle, sharing the best of the cards we found with one another. Laughter was truly healing to the soul.

This is what I would remember most, and miss the most, about our brother. His ability to face life with all of its uncertainties with humor and unmatched wit. He was truly the funniest person I had ever met.

I choked up for a minute and then shook myself to pull it together. *Be strong, Vanessa. Be strong.*

Stephanie finished up her memories and thoughts of my brother, and we walked back to our seats together. More family shared their stories and the pastor closed out the service. We escaped to the back room as per the usual with families at a funeral, but it felt wrong to hide out. I wanted to thank the people who had come. I wanted them to know that we saw them and we appreciated them. Anything to not sit and reflect on what was really going on.

So that is what we did. We smiled and took pictures and thanked people. That is what it looks like to be tough, isn't it?

- - - - - - - -

If I could go back and smack myself, I would. Truly. I would tell myself to not be ridiculous and let my sister cry. To weep and scream if she needed because what we were facing was hard and I had it all wrong.

I Had It All Wrong.

I did not need to stifle my emotions or shove them in some back corner. I did not need to be the first to rush out and focus on the long journeys that some had to make to be there. I did not need to feel embarrassed when I or one of my family members needed to share with the nail technician or grocery store checkout clerk or random stranger that had the unfortunate luck to sit next to us... anywhere... that my brother died. I did not. Because it wasn't strong or powerful to be emotionless and mentally removed from life. It was a survival mechanism. My survival mechanism. One that just prolonged actually dealing with the mounting grief and anguish that filled my heart.

It would be foolish to think that no one has ever felt this way and that I was alone in my sadness, but despite the resounding loneliness, so many others have walked this road before.

In moments of despair, I love to read Paul's writings. The amount of tragedy that he faced gives me an odd sense of satisfaction. (I dare not say Job because I had only lost a handful of people at variant levels of connectedness, while Job lost literally everyone. Everyone except the one nagging wife of course that might have made it easier should she have been engulfed too. Maybe that is why Satan left her alone. I dare not try to find consolation with his story. There is nowhere near comparison. Paul has always been a safer yet still unreachable bet. So this is where I find myself.)

Flipping through Paul's letter to the Corinthians, I came across this large account of the suffering he endured.

He writes:
To my shame, I must say, we were too weak for that! But whatever anyone else dares to boast of—I am speaking as a fool—I also dare to boast of that. Are they Hebrews? So am I. Are they Israelites? So am I. Are they offspring of Abraham? So am I. Are they servants of Christ? I am a better one—I am talking like a madman—with far greater labors, far more imprisonments, with countless beatings, and often near death. Five times I received at the hands of the Jews the forty lashes less one. Three times I was beaten with rods. Once I was stoned. Three times I was shipwrecked; a night and a day I was adrift at sea; on frequent journeys, in danger from rivers, danger from robbers, danger from my own people, danger from Gentiles, danger in the city, danger in the wilderness, danger at sea, danger from false brothers; in toil and hardship, through many a sleepless night, in hunger and thirst, often without food, in cold and exposure. And, apart from other things, there is the daily pressure on me of my anxiety for all the churches.

(2 Corinthians 11:21–28)

Paul, the man who wrote most of the New Testament, the pillar of faith and reason the gospel spread to Asia and Africa, is writing about suffering and hardship *and pressure and anxiety.*

I am not sure why this gives me comfort but it does. Much like the image of Jesus crying out loud in the last chapter.

The idea of strength that I have carried around with me is steady, emotionally untouched, and resolute. Which is why I literally told my sister to stop crying because in order to be strong, she couldn't be allowed to "feel" pain.

She could experience it but not express it.

What a total lie, but it came so quickly that somewhere along the way I must have believed it.

But I am not buying it anymore.

I reject the solemn woman doing all the things despite her world crashing down around her unphased by the damage being done.

And while I still might think it funny, I do not believe the captain of the Titanic yelling "this is fine, everything is fine" a great depiction of who I want to be in this life. That is not strong.

Instead I want to be like Paul who continues on to say, after his extensive lists of heartbreaks and tales of suffering:

Who is weak, and I am not weak? Who is made to fall, and I am not indignant? If I must boast, I will boast of the things that show my weakness.

(2 CORINTHIANS 11:29)

Not because I wish to be weak but because our flesh *is* weak. It is only through Christ that we find real strength. Any strength found outside of that empowered to us by the Holy Spirit is faulty and will not withstand the unrelenting attacks that will come our way. It's a guarantee. We don't have it "in us"—we find it "in Him."

So maybe our new picture of strength should be Jesus being in anguish and crying out to God or Paul stressed out from immeasurable tension and carrying anxiety, because in their fleshly weakness, God was strong. It is not one or the other. It is leaning into the pain and leaning into Him when we feel our lowest, because at that moment we have found the strongest, most secure place. Paul puts it this way just one chapter later:

So to keep me from becoming conceited because of the surpassing greatness of the revelations, a thorn was given me in the flesh, a messenger of Satan to harass me, to keep me from becoming conceited. Three times I pleaded with the Lord about this, that it should leave me. But he said to me, 'My grace is sufficient for you, for my power is made perfect in weakness.' Therefore I will boast all the more gladly of my weaknesses, so that the power of Christ may rest upon me. For the sake of Christ, then, I am content with weaknesses, insults, hardships, persecutions, and calamities. For when I am weak, then I am strong.

(2 CORINTHIANS 12:7–10)

What does this mean for me then? Do I allow myself to be swept up in the emotional roller coaster of grief? Do I give in to the darkness and make my bed in the pit? Of course not.

I am just not glorifying my detachment any longer.

Instead I will embrace where I am in the process and use *what-the-what* all day long to make sure that I continue to lean into Him for sustenance.

Yes you will still find me crying at my desk when that one person walks in with the same walk that my brother had. And yes you will still hear me over-sharing the daylights out of our circumstances and fiery new trials. But you will also see me get out of bed with intention and empowerment from the Lord knowing that I will not let any bit of it keep me down.

The sadness doesn't make me weak, I am weak already. The sadness was what led me to find my real strength in Him after all.

be mindful and realistic about where you are – and then pray for God's strength!

Watch and pray that you may not enter into temptation.

The spirit indeed is willing, but the flesh is weak.

(MATTHEW 26:41)

CHAPTER ELEVEN

I can control my story, not my circumstances

Saturday, June 9, 2018: Rich and I made our way into the large auditorium of the church in Modesto, CA, where our mentor and friend Donnie Moore would be memorialized. The dramatic emotional throat punches we received on repeat were uncanny. Everything started out well enough with a wedding, but the following three Saturdays were one tragedy to the next—an accident, a funeral, and now this. Another memorial service for someone we loved.

I joked that we were taking the next weekend off from life-changing events, but I was only half-kidding while still partly holding my breath. I didn't want to say anything was for certain anymore.

As more and more friends and family filled the seats, I took a poll on just how much devastation was blanketed across the sea of faces. And then I looked to the family who had to stand on the stage and do the same song and dance that I had done just a week prior. I found myself saying how I couldn't imagine their pain. And it was true, I couldn't. But I knew pain too.

Exactly the same, only different, my family would say.

We put on our brave faces and made all the small talk. I had just posted a blog about my certainty of God's presence in tragedy just a few days before (something you might remember from one of the first chapters), and to my surprise many had read it. It was encouraging as I reminded myself of the truth of His nearness more and more. How God was still using my shaky voice through devastation I will never know, but I am so thankful that He did. Even if it was just to show the newfound picture of strength I had grabbed hold of.

Rich had lost himself in some conversation, and I had made my way to the end seat of a row with a quick escape, just in case. It was oddly comforting being there as the feeling felt familiar. I wasn't the sad one in the room. The Debby Downer. Everyone was heartbroken.

The mutual feeling of sadness might have made talking more comfortable, but having spent the past two weeks regretting every interaction that ended with a repulsive amount of word-vomit, I opted to stay quiet instead. I was never sure were my grief-brain might lead. Being quiet was also the safest bet because at any time I was unsure if the numbness would finally wear off and my tears would be unending. Which is even more uncomfortable than sad words. No one knows what to do with tears, it felt.

I sat there alone to my thoughts for a few minutes before feeling a tap on my shoulder.

A pastor whom we had known for many years and who was a close friend with the man we came to honor that day had made his way over to the section that I was seated in to tell me how sorry he was for my loss.

I looked into his kind eyes and was so thankful for his genuine concern. They were fixed and sorrowful, and I imagined his own pain was just as great. He had lost a lifetime friend, and despite them not being actual brothers, I knew how that felt.

Trying to stay true to my previous promise to myself about keeping my words at a minimum, I smiled.

Which if you know me didn't last long. As much as I like to believe I can stay uninvolved, I can't help myself, and without even skipping a beat, I said "God saved my brother from death six times throughout his life. Just long enough to let him say the sinner's prayer. I am thankful for your kind words but my brother made it home."

Those words shocked even myself as they left my lips, but they were true nonetheless. It wasn't a reprimand but a testament to God's love and faithfulness even now.

I was sad but God was still in control.

He replied that he didn't know that about my brother, and

I wanted him to understand how I was able to make such a leap. I briefly talked about all of John's near-death experiences and then the triumphant blink he gave us the last day he was responsive. I was still mad, still sad that he was gone, but I couldn't change any of that. What I chose to focus on instead was how God had been faithful all along. Reaching through the darkest of nights for the man who was a far way off.

And now, being as he is no longer here with us, he isn't a far way off anymore.

The man thanked me for sharing John's story with him and he found his way back to his seat. I lowered my head a bit in reflection to think on how all of the tragedies had still left me with this one hope—this one story—and it was the only one worth sharing. Yes, there was still sadness, still a member of our family who would never make it to my parents for Christmas or call to tell us the newest resort his work had brought him to, and still a tightness felt in my chest anytime I would remember him, but there was also still this assurance that God was not on vacation or uncaring in it all.

Rich returned to where we had set down our items and asked that we move a little closer. He guided us to our new seats in the second row on the left hand side quite literally squished between a man and his wife that I have admired in ministry for years and friends from decades past. All in the same boat of shock and grief as we shared more than a professional relation-ship with Donnie and the Moore family but a personal one, too.

There was a good amount of noise in the air. Conversations were being had, hugs shared, and memories flowing. I wasn't ready for all of that as I remained in my seat, snuggly pressed against the back of the pew. I quite literally had made my tall five-foot-nine frame into the smallest proportion that I could make it so that I was not impeding on anyone else's personal space. My own, first of all. This tightened position made a two-hour service fairly uncomfortable, but that day wasn't about me.

We laughed through the memories shared, cried through the videos played, and hugged every last person we knew when it was all said and done.

Life has always been precious, but never before has it been so important to tell others how much they meant to us. We didn't waste it.

- - - - - - - -

Donnie's story is not mine to share. What I can say of this giant of a man is that during my darkest season of life, God chose him to reach me. My life did a complete 180 as I knelt at the altar of the Easter Camp I was gifted a scholarship to that one week back in 2002. I left a world of bitterness, unforgiveness, abuse, pain, and self-harm at the bottom of that stage never to be picked up again. God moved powerfully in my life in the weeks and months to follow, and I never looked back. Because of your obedience to those camps, Donnie, I never turned back.

Years later my husband and I would feel a call to serve him, moving our home and first child to Stockton, CA, to spend a few years helping to build (and bring into the twenty-first century) a ministry that had so profoundly impacted both of our lives. Those years spent with him and his family were irreplaceable. Monday nights soon became our family favorite as we were invited into their home to talk all manners of life over coffee with his wife while all of the guys worked out in the gym he had built in his backyard.

I found more healing and vision for my life at their kitchen counter than anywhere else.

When the Lord prompted us to move three years later to assist with a friend's church plant, we did so through much prayer and a bit of resistance. We knew it was God's plan, but we hated to leave the community that we had formed, especially the Moores. Every last one of them was family.

Looking back on those times and taking an assessment of where we are now, my heart is both heavy and thankful. I watched as our leaving changed so much of how we were perceived by many but how through the years God has restored many of our relationships. I wonder from time to time what our story could have been if God had not intervened and if we had not made an effort to ask forgiveness or forgive where needed. Our account of things past could have shaped our present in a much different way.

This is true of all of us. *Our narratives are our choosing.* They are made up of many parts, but the two I find at the top of the list for "most likely to mess things up" are tragedy and regret.

Some might think what makes a truly good story are those full of tragedy. I agree that all stories of great impact first start at the bottom, but take notice of all of the stories that included loss and then the subsequent spiral downhill of an individual. Not including the moral failures of many who face the consequences of their own actions. That is something else altogether and not what this book is about. We are talking about grief, so let's take a look at that for a minute.

We have ventured through tragedy in many forms: the losses of life through an accident, overdose, suicide, cancer, old age, and more; losses of relationships through divorce in the family, abandonment of responsibilities/relationships, a big move (or three), or offense; and losses of purpose through job loss, relocation, unsupported visions, and financial instability.

A plethora of tragedies, a world of loss, but a choice to have each one change us for better or worse.

All of them painful, all with their own power to mar what we say of God and ourselves. And while we cannot change what happened, we can choose how we see them and what we will speak about them over our lives.

These things did not destroy us.

Say that to yourself. "(Insert whatever you are facing) will not destroy me." Say it out loud and however often you need to say it.

And just as this tragedy will not destroy you, you can choose to not let it define you either. This thing you face is not the anti-hero in the story. It is not the kryptonite being hurled your way. It is not your life's greatest battle. It is what God is using to shape you. It is a terrible thing meant to destroy you forged by the enemy himself but in the right hands will make you exactly who you were intended to be. When we fix our eyes on Jesus, our purposes are not lost in the great pit of despair.

As the old song says, "You can take the whole world, but give me Jesus."

If we weren't living in a fallen world, then I would imagine it to be not so true. But it is. Everything in this world has the potential to be taken, removed, and destroyed.

That is why we cannot build our lives on any one thing, but Him.

Paul experienced much suffering in life but look at what he encourages us to do:

> Indeed, I count everything as loss because of the surpassing worth of knowing Christ Jesus my Lord. For his sake I have suffered the loss of all things and count them as rubbish, in order that I may gain Christ and be

found in him, not having a righteousness of my own that comes from the law, but that which comes through faith in Christ, the righteousness from God that depends on faith—that I may know him and the power of his resurrection, and may share his sufferings, becoming like him in his death, that by any means possible I may attain the resurrection from the dead. Not that I have already obtained this or am already perfect, but I press on to make it my own, because Christ Jesus has made me his own.

(PHILIPPIANS 3:8–12)

That may sound confusing, but what he is saying is this: I have been through it all, victories and defeat, feasting and suffering, and the only thing that matters, the reason I am still living and pushing forward, is the knowledge that I am His. And beyond that, there will be a day when He calls me home and my reward will be complete. I will finish my race that day, gaining Heaven as my new home, and finally understand what all of the struggle was meant to keep me from.

Because we are not fighting against "flesh and blood" as it says in Ephesians. We are fighting an enemy who wants to quite literally "annihilate" us from humanity as if we never existed. That is what the word "destroy" in John 10:10, "the thief comes only to steal and kill and destroy," translates to. The Devil, Satan, or Beelzebub, whatever you want to call him, hates you and wants nothing more than to separate you from a loving God and a fulfilling life. Don't let him.

Choose instead to rise and rise again declaring the words God chose to finish that same verse with, "I came that they may have life and have it abundantly."

Beyond tragedies not of our making, another powerful

force has the ability to change our stories, and that is the regret we face in the wake of devastation.

I wish I would have called more often to express how much the Moore family had shaped our lives. Still today I wish I could communicate things that were left unsaid so many years ago. And not just with Donnie but my brother also. Had I known he was going to die, I would have told him how incredible he was and how thankful I am to be his sister. I would have snuck in that piece of pizza that he so desperately wanted to eat because he was going to pass anyway.

Ok, maybe I wouldn't have snuck in the pizza, but I might have highly considered it.

These looming ideas of unsaid words or unshown love and appreciation have the ability to change everything. Most importantly, the stories we share. They taint every word, emotion, and memory because regret has no end.

I wonder what beauty we can find when we remove it from our vocabulary. What would happen if we chose instead to focus on the facts, taking out any "should haves" or "would haves" to look at a story through the lens of what is?

In our own story, I often thought in the beginning how I should have noticed my brother's lung capacity decreasing over the course of our one night spent together. It was during our last sleepover that the infection became rampant in his body, and I would be lying if I said I haven't thought about what would have happened if I had alerted a nurse to the unsettling sounds I was hearing or the silly cough that wasn't doing much. In the moment I told myself that I was not a trained professional, but the regret of not understanding what was happening could have been crippling if I allowed myself to walk down that road.

We cannot do this to ourselves.

We cannot change what was.

Paul continues to write the same thing to the Philippians in his letter as he urges them to stop looking back. He says it this way:

Brothers, I do not consider that I have made it my own. But one thing I do: forgetting what lies behind and straining forward to what lies ahead, I press on toward the goal for the prize of the upward call of God in Christ Jesus.

(PHILIPPIANS 3:13–14)

If we are to lay hold of the prize, our eternal salvation, and share in the call of the Great Commission by helping others know Him, then we must do so with both eyes looking ahead.

I understand how hard this can be. I know the guilt and pain of regret, not like you as you venture your own dark road, but I understand how crippling it can be. It feels impossible, but it's not.

Change the one thing you have the power to change, your words, and just watch how your story unfolds.

It will still be full of tragedy and suffering, but the ending will be the best part. The one that shows your giving God free reign to redeem and rework every bit of it for your benefit. If you paid so great a price for anything else, wouldn't you want to stick around for the reward? Now is your chance. It's coming. I promise, it is coming.

New hope and new dreams will be birthed out of your greatest pains. This present darkness may have fooled us for a moment, but the morning will come again. And when it does, we will be ready.

If you are in that place of deep regret, please know that I

am praying healing over you. For God to show Himself strong on your behalf and remove those deep pangs of failure or loss, replacing them with peace and strength to carry on with Him and through Him. Hang on. Don't let go. Our Redeemer lives.

Rejoice in the Lord always; again I will say, rejoice. Let

your reasonableness be known to everyone. The Lord is

at hand; do not be anxious about anything, but in

everything by prayer and supplication with thanksgiving

let your requests be made known to God. And the peace

of God, which surpasses all understanding, will guard

your hearts and your minds in Christ Jesus. Finally,

brothers, whatever is true, whatever is honorable,

whatever is just, whatever is pure, whatever is lovely,

whatever is commendable, if there is any excellence, if

there is anything worthy of praise, think about these

things. What you have learned and received and heard

and seen in me—practice these things, and the God of

peace will be with you.

(PHILIPPIANS 4:4-9)

thought
checklist:
0 is it true
0 is it honorable
0 is it just
0 is it pure
0 is it lovely
0 is it commendable
0 is it excellent

142

the sun will shine again

Saturday, April 27, 2019: Stephanie clutched the small speckled orange glass jar in her palms pressing her lips to its exterior as tears rolled down her cheeks. She was a sight to behold. Her fiery red hair flowed across her mermaid-style long-sleeved white dress like a princess from one of our children's books. It would have been nothing short of a fairytale had it not been for the presence of the sinking feelings of incompleteness that loomed in the stale summery air. The stale summery ninety-seven-degree air. God, help us.

We didn't all make it to the orchard to see Stephanie say "I do." We didn't all make it to watch her glide down the aisle, smiling ear to ear as she held tightly to my father's arm. We didn't all make it.

Knowing that our family would inevitably be missing the most beautifully bearded Benbow of the bunch (yes I understand that John was the only boy in the family whom would naturally be assumed to grow strong facial hair, but us girls have Lebanese roots and cannot be counted out), my mother brought her small urn with my brother's ashes. She just wanted to feel like he could be there. Like he wasn't missing out on this huge family milestone. That *we* weren't missing out.

I choked back tears as my mother pulled it out and had to look away when it was time for Stephanie to have a moment with "John." Oh, to be a fly on the wall in that RV-turned dressing room while Stephanie whispered words to our brother on her wedding day. I never asked what she spoke into the air. What she spoke to John. But I knew it was their little secret.

The photographer finished up, and we dashed to the back of the aisle as the processional was about to start. I shifted my mind to anything but the image that I had just seen and told myself to breathe. There was no hiding the absence of what we lost, but a wedding is an opportunity for celebration. John would have wanted us to focus on that.

I stood up tall, just shy of the groomsman who escorted me in my three-and-a-half-inch heels and set my eyes to the finish line.

"You look great Stephanie," Rich who again was officiating the wedding said with sincerity then turned his attention toward the groom.

"Eh, you look alright Harmony," he joked as he pretended to lick his thumb and wipe a spot away on his bald head. Everyone laughed. Rich was so proud of himself.

I heard him rehearsing that line the night before, so I just smiled as I looked down at my shoes. That man is such a goober and I love him for it. He knew exactly how hard this day would be and handled it with gentleness and fun. I have a sneaking suspicion that John would have gotten a kick out of it all.

The sun beat down on us unhindered as Rich spoke words of love and commitment. The happy couple exchanged their own vows. Stephanie had written a few sentences down while Harmony spoke eloquently from his heart, words he no doubt had repeated over and over in his head the last few days as they came without hesitation or pause.

I thought to myself how the day might have gone should our family have decided instead to drag our feet and be upset with the world. What would have happened if we allowed John's absence to destroy us and suck the joy out of the moment?

Would we have laughed at the corny jokes or noticed the soft sun resting on the cheeks of the guests, some of whom had driven hours to join us that day? Would we have given ourselves permission to dance and share toasts and eat way too many tacos?

What would this wedding day, another sister's wedding, look like had one or all of us chosen to not have another good day? Because we could have. We could very well have chosen that there would never again be reason to sing or celebrate. That what was missing, what was taken, was too much making it impossible to experience happiness again.

The thought came flooding into my mind as I looked around to take it all in. We could have missed *this*.

This the celebration of two people committing their lives to one another. This the reunion of friends and family from around the country. This the joy and merriment of officially welcoming another brother to the brood. We could have missed it in our missing.

Now I do not claim to be a professional at what it looks like to keep moving forward. I still cried during my toast that I had written out to prevent such a thing and most of the way on our six-hour drive home for that matter. I still have hard days and am sometimes triggered by sirens, hospitals, and pictures of accidents. But in spite of it all, the toggling between peace and sadness (and sometimes peace during sadness), I have embraced that the potential still exists to have more good days.

Truth be told, each moment has the possibility to be your next favorite memory. Even though you are still hurting. And just as much as it is possible for it to be your next favorite, this next memory you create also has the potential to be your last.

I thank God that as of now, we still have our family intact a handful of weeks later. It is a morbid thought to actually draw attention to this detail, but the last time that we had a wedding, we had a funeral two weeks later.

And while this correlation could have prevented me from putting on another bridesmaids dress and walking down another aisle, it actually had the opposite effect. It made me appreciate every new opportunity as something I might cherish forever for being both my new favorite and my last.

This is life. No matter if we are standing thirty feet tall (like how I imagined myself to look next to Bethany, my youngest sister, that day… who wore flats in her dress… already being significantly shorter than Stephanie and I) or cowering in some corner somewhere. It keeps moving. Keeps affording more opportunities for beauty and tragedy.

We chose to take the chance and showed up knowing it could be both.

- - - - - - - -

I meant to leave things with the last day of our marathon of Saturdays of sadness, but I couldn't walk away from this one last truth, because it is the most important lesson that I have learned in the process of walking around in the dark.

No matter how hard and how bleak it gets, the sun (read Son) *will* shine again.

The morning light will slowly creep into the night and touch the dark places with a warmth that they had been without for too long. Or just long enough, it turns out. Maybe not now, maybe not next week, but eventually you will wake up and your pillow won't be soaked with tears. Eventually you will share a memory, and it won't cause the darkness to creep back in. Eventually the loss you now carry will just make you a better more beautiful person, and not just more broken.

Eventually.

Elisabeth Kübler-Ross, a Swiss-American psychiatrist who came up with the theory on the five stages of grief, once said: "The most beautiful people we have known are those who have known defeat, known suffering, known struggle, known loss, and have found their way out of the depths. These persons have an appreciation, a sensitivity, and an understanding of life that fills them with compassion, gentleness, and a deep loving concern. Beautiful people do not just happen" (Kübler-Ross 1975).

This will be us, my friends. The kind people. The empathetic people. The compassionate people. The beautiful people. Not despite our pain but because of it.

I cannot say that I am fully there yet, but I trust that one day I will learn to live inside of this new normal committed to finding the new beauty in it. Not because I have "gotten over" it. There is no such thing. But because God has walked with me through the darkest parts of the journey already.

And when the shadowy figures turn back into familiar objects and faces, you too will find your way beyond the place you now find yourself in. You just will.

You will find a way to remember the tragedy and ever-faithful guidance of a loving God like Joshua walking through the Jordan River with the entire nation of Israel following behind him, relying solely on Him for their survival. Do you remember this story? The story of God's chosen people? The ones who complained and turned their backs and wrestled with God's faithfulness time and time again, and yet God chose to never desert them. Twice He parted the waters for His chosen people to walk through. Twice.

I love this story because it is our story. The ones we venture through in loss when at every turn we think this new thing will be the one that kills us. We think to ourselves, *we can't do it. We can't go on.* And God in His great love makes a new way that could never have existed before. The waters part, the grounds clear, and God gently encourages us to go just a little further.

If I were to imagine where I was right now in this journey, I would say somewhere in the middle of the Jordan River. I hope you read that as dramatic and sarcastic as I wrote it. Because at times, I legitimately feel like I am in the middle of the river.

Not drowning of course, despite the intended imagery. No, God has stopped its raging and stored up its waters long enough for me to walk this road, thinking all along that at any moment I could very well be swallowed up whole should I tarry too long in my wandering. I mean, we aren't talking forty years like the Israelites with the crossing of the Jordan River being the last step before entering their Promised Land (*despite not being an entire generation not able to enter it at all because of their unfaithful-ness*), but this last year has felt like forty at times.

The most incredible part of this story isn't even the miracle of God pushing back the waters. To me, the really life-impacting image is that of the twelve leaders of the tribes of Judah stooping down in the middle of the river bed to pick up a *dry* rock.

Proof, they were picking up proof of God's faithfulness to them.

And that's what these lessons have been for me all along—dry rocks.

Something to hold close and remind me of the times when God was faithful when everything seemed futile. When the world was closing in and I was staring at the great unknown wondering how I would arrive anywhere else than the place I am now. The place you find yourself in. The place you were sure would destroy you. But at just the right time, the Lord sent word and made a way.

This is the Israelites' story, but this is our story, too. We know what it is to feel hopeless and at a dead end. We know that constant pressing from all sides. And still, God makes a way where we thought it impossible to make a way. Where we said we'd never be able to move beyond, God clears the path and sends His presence on ahead so we never have to walk it alone.

One foot in front of the other. One day, sometimes one moment, at a time.

Just read this passage of the story as Joshua leads the charge following the death of his close mentor, Moses (yes, remember Joshua was leading an entire nation bearing his own grief):

Then Joshua called the twelve men from the people of Israel, whom he had appointed, a man from each tribe. And Joshua said to them, 'Pass on before the ark of the LORD your God into the midst of the Jordan, and take up each of you a stone upon his shoulder, according to the number of the tribes of the people of Israel, that this may be a sign among you. When your children ask in time to come, 'What do those stones mean to you?' then you shall tell them that the waters of the Jordan were cut off before the ark of the covenant of the LORD. When it passed over the Jordan, the waters of the Jordan were cut off. So these stones shall be to the people of Israel a memorial forever. And the people of Israel did just as Joshua commanded and took up twelve stones out of the midst of the Jordan, according to the number of the tribes of the people of Israel, just as the LORD told Joshua. And they carried them over with them to the place where they lodged and laid them down there.

(JOSHUA 4:4–8)

When they ask, and they will, one day soon you will be able to say that you made it to the other side. You are still grieving, still always wishing that your loved one was here, but you aren't covered in darkness anymore. It isn't painstakingly difficult to get out of bed or remind yourself that there is still purpose in this life. Because you found it again.

I wasn't sure at first.

Oftentimes I would find myself saying over and over, in a joking way, "I don't like it here." I might have said it a few too many times as a close friend ended up making me a shirt with that very thing written on it. I laughed because it was exactly what I felt. It was my new life motto. I just wanted to go home. And by home I meant the one where there was no weeping or gnashing of teeth. When the pain ceases and it is just an eternity of joy.

I smile when I wear that shirt now. (Around the house of course because could you imagine me wearing it in public? At a restaurant, someone's house, or, God forbid, church? People wouldn't understand that my "here" is anywhere that isn't Heaven. Because I surely didn't want to be anywhere but there.)

Life got too hard, too much of a burden, too dark for me to want to be on earth any longer. And while I didn't dare venture into suicidal ideation territory, thanks to God Himself, I wouldn't have been upset either if the Lord had decided that it was my time too.

I *didn't* like it here.

But I do now.

I am thankful now.

I can see the Promised Land in the distance now. The rocks I now carry can attest. Each one I gathered along the way.

They are for me, but they are for my kids too. The ones with the front row seat to what it looks like to lose someone. The ones who were unsure if mommy was going to make it out. If she was "okay." The ones who still look at me a little crazy when I wear that silly shirt with a smile on my face. Because it doesn't make any sense. I wear it still. It reminds me of the girl who was in the thick of it. It reminds me of how far God has brought me. And it reminds me of all He has taught me in the midst of my pain.

By the time the morning light had come, it was just me in this silly shirt carrying some dry rocks that have now become the most treasured thing I have ever owned. They are the proof that, despite popular belief, God is still good. Even in the messy stuff. These rocks are my victory. For me and my household and anyone who might wander into our lives.

Even more than that, the rocks are for you.

For the days when you wonder if you will ever get out of bed again, ever find hope or love again, and ever trust that God is good or near again. When you are at your darkest, I hope you remember my unexpected gifts of the darkness.

There are things about Him that we can only learn when we are at the bottom of a pit, on a cold dark day, completely surrounded. When you find yourself in that place, look for Him there.

Look for God in the darkness.

And bring a pen and paper, as you never know what treasure hunt the Lord might send you on while you are at the bottom on your way back up. God won't waste your journey.

bonus material

A small collection of helpful tools to offer insight into what you can say (or should not say) and what you can do to offer support to those who are enduring the loss of a loved one.

Please note that I am not an expert and this is not an extensive list, but it has been confirmed by my tribe of fellow sojourners, and we agree that the world could use having them written down and be read.

Not because people are evil or uncaring, but because they just don't know how to respond. I pray this helps answer that question.

what to say to a grieving person

Please don't take this as a manifesto or a list of offenses I have picked up along the way. These lists are simply my thoughts on how we can be better co-burden carriers to make things a little easier for those who wish to share their love and concern with those trudging through loss.

1. "I am sorry for your loss."

Do not underestimate this expression. Yes it is the go-to for doctors and counselors and pastors alike, but for good reason. You are acknowledging what a person has just gone through without hyper-sensationalizing it or making it of no importance. This comment is sincere and to the point. Hearing it a thousand times is better than hearing a thousand different things.

2. "You don't have to respond..."

When someone walks through grief, they are walking around in the densest of fogs. This means that nine times out of ten, if not more (for those of us math wizards that means 10/10), texts, phone calls, and emails will go unanswered. By prefacing a message with "you don't have to respond" or "please don't feel you need to respond," you are saying that your concern is strictly for them. That you understand and want to relay your love for them without that person also carrying the weight of needing to reciprocate any attention. That your friendship is more than just give and take, but in the truly difficult times it is receiving when there is nothing left to give. Please be this friend. (BTW please don't call. Just don't. Talking is too much.)

3. "I love you."

Those three words can break through the loneliness that grief often subjects onto a person and allow them to feel like they can breathe again, just by being "seen" and still cherished despite feeling like a void of a person. Love speaks life back into the broken and hurting.

4. "What do you need?" (and mean it)

Now I know that this is more than just words, at least I hope, but so many may not know how to help a grieving person. Mostly because when asked, a person will reply, "nothing" or "just pray." But truth be told, there are some things that make a world of difference when someone is struggling to get out of bed in the morning. So to those who offer and have the ability to follow through, thank you! You will never know the strength and relief you offer, if only for a moment.

5. "I am praying for you."

(Bonus points to include the things you are praying for and Scriptures where God promises those things to us.)

This is not just cliché Christian rhetoric—or at least it shouldn't be. We should be praying for one another both out loud and in our quiet places. Texts that express friends are praying and specifically what they are saying on my behalf are incredible and life-giving! I can never express my appreciation for those who spoke the Word over me and over our situation. The Scriptures are alive and powerful, just like it describes in Hebrews 4:12, so using them do more for a situation than we can ever do on our own. Thank you to everyone who offered a prayer on our behalf, both publicly and privately. We may not even know each other's names, but I can assure you that God heard every word.

I would also like to caution this with a big red flag: do not, in any case, express that you are praying for a person without checking with them that it is what they are also believing God for. Just please. If they post something public and ask for prayers of healing, then pray that. If they are asking for peace, pray that. If there are no specific things posted, then text them that you are praying, and whatever your personal feelings are, whatever things you are desiring to see in their situation, pray specifically to the Father for those.

It is incredibly painful in moments of great sadness to hear or read that friends are praying in a way that is not in alignment with your own prayers.

Yes, a grieving person may not have the faith for miracles. And yes, sometimes their prayers seem small in comparison to the need. But responding with a one-upper or in "arrogant" faith pushes that person further away as it causes feelings like they are not a "good enough" Christian to believe for the big stuff. I could write a whole book (ok maybe a pamphlet) on how damaging this can be, especially when it is done publicly and you have unbelieving family members who gain false hope and when God doesn't answer how it was presented are now faced with believing that God doesn't exist, that God doesn't care, or that prayer doesn't work.

If you are believing for a miracle and it isn't in alignment with someone who is suffering, write it down. Write it down so you can show them when God answers—because yes, He is still alive, He does love us, and He still answers prayer. This would mean more to a person than parading your faith in front of them, even if the result was the same.

what not to say to a grieving person

If someone's life is on fire, don't mix up the water and gasoline. There are many more things that can bring life in situations of death, but there are also some incredibly damaging words that are often given to an already hurting person. And in an effort to prevent more insult to injury from happening, please read over these next eight things to prepare yourself for how to best approach the loss of life with a loved one. (And please hear my heart on these, I promise we all have done it.)

1. Nothing.

We all grew up with the "if you don't have anything nice to say, don't say anything at all," thinking that silence was far better than negativity. And I agree. But silence is also *the worst* thing. With grief, silence from those you thought were friends is just as bad as a negative comment. I am so serious. Say something. Say the smallest of things. Just say something. Don't go radio silent or dark or invisible when someone is dealing with loss. It hurts. So bad, it hurts.

2. "God will _____."

This goes along with what we talked about above—we do not know what God *will* do. We are not fortune tellers. Yes, I do acknowledge/understand/appreciate that God gives the gift of prophecy. I love this about Him. I love this about His people. But more times than not, this is not what I have witnessed walking through storms myself or with people. People have used *"God will"* for *"I want"* and end up doing more damage in the Lord's name than they realize. As I mentioned before, write it down. I still believe you can have BIG faith and pray BIG prayers and hear BIG things. I just want to also express how those things can be received without damaging a person's faith or hopeful faith.

3. *"It was God's Will."*

This can be very confusing for a new believer or unbeliever as they hear that "it is God's will to heal them" and then in the next breath "it was God's will for them to pass." God was not confused. In the matter of death, death was never God's "will." In fact it was never in the original design. Now that sin is here, He is desperate for us to find salvation so that we may have eternal *life* once and for all. Scripture says "The Lord is not slack concerning His promise, as some count slackness, but is longsuffering toward us, not willing that any should perish but that all should come to repentance" (2 Peter 3:9). And not just with death, but with serious illness or injury or outcome; please do not revert back to it all being "God's will" even if you believe it to be. Some things are more about our choices than God's will.

4. *"Everything happens for a reason."*

This is not scriptural. I'm sorry if you were never told or realized this. Scripturally it says that God will turn our ashes into beauty and that He will redeem *all*. The Bible says "And we know that all things work together for good to those who love God, to those who are the called according to His purpose" (Romans 8:28). The word "work" is placed in this verse for a reason, because sometimes life gives God a lot of things to work with to make things work for our benefit. It takes work. It was not a thought-out poop-shoot to rain on your parade. But don't be dismayed. God is working all the things for your benefit.

5. *"God needed them more."*

This one hurts so much and I could go the rest of my life without hearing it again. Everyone's life will end in death. This is true. But God is not in a hurry and doesn't "need" people in heaven when they are faithfully serving His purposes on this earth. He *wants* them, yes! But ours is the need.

Paul said it best when he said:

For I know that this will turn out for my deliverance through your prayer and the supply of the Spirit of Jesus Christ, according to my earnest expectation and hope that in nothing I shall be ashamed, but with all boldness, as always, so now also Christ will be magnified in my body, whether by life or by death. For to me, to live is Christ, and to die is gain... For I am hard-pressed between the two, having a desire to depart and be with Christ, which is far better. Nevertheless to remain in the flesh is more needful for you. (Philippians 1:19–24)

6. "What happened??"

Inquiring the story of what became the ultimate demise of a person you loved is basically the worst. Please don't. I understand our curiosity gets the better of us, but let's learn from the cat. Or the dog who decided to eat the cat's poop who is now sick in my house.... If the story was meant to be shared, it would have been. Let the grieving person share it when they are ready.

7. "I know exactly how you feel."

I want to tread lightly here because I do not want to diminish anyone's feelings of loss as it is a universal thing. But friends, please do not take the opportunity to share your personal story of grief with a person who has newly lost someone. It does not feel encouraging. In fact, being told that someone "knows exactly how they feel" is rarely true because like the grief process, grief itself is very unique to the person. No two stories are exactly the same.

The only time it is appropriate to swap stories is when a grieving person decides to attend a support group to talk through their hurt and find comradery. Very rarely does this happen right away.

A person who is in mourning would rather not talk about it or only talk about his own loss. In the grief process, they should be allowed to grieve how they feel they need to grieve, as long as it is not detrimental to their health or well-being. Please let them set the parameters and share their story without feeling like they have to compete with your hurt. (I would like to add that this is something I have been notorious for, and only through my own loss have I learned to stay quiet and not jump in with my own experiences unless asked. I am sorry for every time I have unknowingly done this and want to spare others the same remorse.)

8. *"Aren't you over it yet?"*

I'm just going to pause a moment to thank the Lord for letting me never have to personally experience this question. I know it was for their protection and my freedom from imprisonment that you have kept this from being uttered in my presence, Father. Thank you.

But for the few whom have shared receiving this question, this is for you. I am sorry you ever had to hear it.

I just can't with this, and I hope you understand why because I don't even have the emotional stability to explain.

Please don't.

what you can do for a grieving person

To anyone who has a loved one that has lost someone, I want to share a few ways that you can help... even though when you ask they will say "nothing"... because they either are overwhelmed with how much there is to do and can't pin point one thing, or they don't want to feel like an inconvenience. Either way, I have asked some friends whom have recently lost family members, and we have come up with a short list of thirteen great ways that you can prove that love is an action word!

1. *Be available and present*

When we first got the call that my brother had been in an accident, it was like the worst kind of adrenaline rush. Everything was going a mile a minute and it was hard to keep up. And then, as if all of a sudden and yet ever so slightly, time stood still. It was hard to keep track of the days as they continued rolling on despite our not leaving the hospital or finding anywhere to sleep for more than a few hours at a time. Each day felt like an eternity that would never end as we waited for any kind of news or change. The only thing that broke up the waiting game were the few close friends and family members that would pop in to join us from time to time.

Our family limited the amount of visitors we had to protect our time together and those who process differently in our little group, as it should be, but when you are trudging through dark waters and have been staring at the same people for a few days with little sleep or appetite, it doesn't hurt to mix it up.

And it isn't just in a waiting room that you can offer your company—being "available" for many of the other things listed below is just as impactful. Show up to the funeral even if it is just to offer a short hug or smile across the room. Make an effort to just "be there" for all of the plans, or to make none of them, because being there is one of the best things that you can do.

(I want to share a disclaimer that each individual will vary drastically in how much they want to "people" in the midst of tragedy. Please ask ahead of time if your close friend—and I say "close" very intentionally here—would like company and put a time limit on it.)

2. Buy gift cards (and other items)

This was our family's personal favorite as our mood for company would change from moment to moment (most of the time depending on the newest update that we were receiving). For everyone who bought our family a gift card, *thank you!* Seriously, you will never know the true beauty of not having to look at your bank account to determine if you need to hit a dollar menu or can actually sit down when you want to get away for a while.

A few places that are extremely helpful for those looking to purchase a gift card are the hospital cafeteria (did you know you can buy a gift card to those?! Incredible!!!), coffee stores/restaurants near where the family is staying, gas cards or hotel vouchers for family traveling long distances, or a gift card to Target/Walmart for last-minute purchases.

Bonus Idea: One firefighter who had recently lost a child dropped off a tub of necessities that became a huge help. The tub included tissues, trash bags, paper plates, napkins, plastic utensils, toilet paper, and paper towels. Everything a family might need when not wanting to wash dishes or run errands while they process their loss. Gifts of this nature are a God send because you never think of how taxing cleaning your house or cooking for your family can be until getting out of bed is an award-winning achievement. Another bonus idea: Our family was given a teddy bear from John's place of work that meant *so much* to my mother, and I was personally given a necklace that reads "Hope." These are both beautiful reminders that we can carry with us through the hard days.

3. Run errands

Despite a grieving person's world coming to a standstill, the rest of the world does not. Bills still need to be paid, children still need to be dropped off at school, and laundry still needs to be done. Making yourself available to run around town, pick up items from their house, or wash a person's laundry so they don't have to "inside outside" (if you know what I mean) is a HUGE help! Even going grocery shopping for that person can mean the world. Some people want to get outside and get back to doing normal things and that is great, but for many meaningless errands are just too much.

4. Drop off food/coffee

My personal response to stress, and life really, is to drink all the coffee and save the food for happier times, but this is not universal. Some people *cough dad* prefer to slowly nervous eat their way through stress. Sometimes stopping for fast food that makes you want to vomit in the back seat, hypothetically of course. For the eaters out there, bravo for being able to take care of yourself! I'll just take all the coffee, please.

On a serious note, we had a handful of family friends who drop off food while we stayed in the hospital. Some to my family who was still in San Luis Obispo (*thank you friends!*) and some to us in the ICU. It was a blessing all around. An extra big thank you to those who speak my love language and kept the coffee coming! Especially with the hospital vending machine spitting out something that looked and tasted like muddy poop water. My cousin had a name for it in fact; I won't share that here.

While homemade food and beefed up sandwiches were the best-tasting thing we had had all week, a few times we just couldn't imagine eating and let some of the food go to waste. For a bonus idea, you can drop off nonperishable items for families to keep around such as protein bars, trail mix, bottled waters, fruit, chips, and the like. (*We had one family add chocolate to their bag of goodies—you're my people.*) And one more bonus idea: freeze all the homemade things, and drop it off for the person once they return home to reheat whenever they are up to eating!!! Yay for not having to cook or eating PB&J again!

5. Help tie up loose ends

While I would love to say that the loss of life is just processing grief and crying whenever and for whatever reason, the truth is that it involves a lot of work. This person occupied a room or a house, had animals, and had maybe even a few unfinished business items.

I hate this part.

I wish I could have jumped in to help after things were settled, but I did not. I had to drive five hours away to go back to work and left my father and sisters to do the heavy lifting. They are my heroes. They did the hard things, but thankfully they did not have to do it all alone.

For those who might not have known, my parents moved to our neck of the woods just the day before the accident, and my brother intended to rent our family home. After he passed, my parents decided to move forward with putting that house on the market which meant boxing up All. The. Things. and cleaning every inch of that house. Then there was the loading/unloading and driving of said boxes down to SLO. My husband sent me a picture an hour in to the packing and said that there were over thirty people from the Sacramento Fire Department there with more on their way (momentary pause for how much I still tear up when I acknowledge this).

Being able to pack boxes, drive a U-Haul, clean a house, or lift heavy items are all wonderful ways you can help tie up loose ends, but there are also other things that are helpful too. Some people aren't as technology-inclined and need help downloading pictures and voicemails from a phone, closing out social media accounts, or stripping a computer to resell. There is also the task of selling some items online and repurposing items (such as making a quilt out of old clothes) that are wonderful ways to make a terrible situation a little less terrible.

6. Offer your services for funeral arrangements

There are precisely one million things to do in a short amount of time, and if you have certain skills, you can help!

If you are a pastor, you can offer grief counseling or offer to do the service. If you are a graphic designer, you can design the funeral program. If you are familiar with video programs, you can put together the picture montage. If you are a florist, you can offer flowers at a discounted rate. If you are a baker, you can offer bringing items to the reception (if they are having one). If you are a caterer, you can offer providing food at a discounted rate (or in our case, you can have the incredible people at Ingram Eatz located in Roseville, CA, feed our entire family at no charge— *please give them your business!*). If you are a creative person, you might even offer to display the pictures in a beautiful way or help with the guest table.

There are so many ways to help, so if you are close to the family and want to pitch in instead of saying "whatever you need," try saying "I would love to help with (insert service you can offer here), if you don't have someone in mind already."

7. Help promote/give toward a GoFundMe or other fundraising account

I cannot even begin to explain the pain that is paying for a person you loved to be cremated or buried. Or what it feels like to get a bill for the storage unit that holds all of a person's belongings that you can't get to just yet. Even worse, the hospital bill for all of the efforts made to keep your loved one here just one more day. And these are just three of the many financial responsibilities that pile up during a loss. If a person shares a fundraising account, share it and give (if even $20) toward it. Everything helps.

One of my favorite examples of this type of community sharing is found in Acts 2 when it says "Now all who believed were together, and had all things in common, and sold their possessions and goods, and divided them among all, as anyone had need" (verses 44–45). Man, what it would look like to go without a few coffees or sell an old piece of furniture or something that truly requires a sacrifice because someone has a need. If at the very least, we can share a post to give others the opportunity.

8. *Put reminders in your phone to reach out once a week*

I wish I could say that grief stops when the service ends but that is just not real life. However, for many friends after the funeral is over, it is "out of sight out of mind." A beautiful way to support a loved one is by setting a reminder to check in each week or every few weeks. Believe me, they haven't forgotten or moved on. They are still very much in the thick of it, and a quick "thinking of you today and praying over you still"(or something a little longer like a special friend of mine sent a few weeks after) goes a long way. The really hard emotions don't even start until the numbness wears off and you are two to three months down the road. Of course this is also when life is back in full swing and you sound like a broken record if you say out loud that you are hurting. Because yes, we are still hurting.

If you are the encouraging or thoughtful type, this is a huge way to be a help. Because we need it. All the texts and all the prayers (which just so happens to be #9.) There has never been a checkup text that I have regretted receiving... even if it still takes me a week to respond.

If you do decide to reach out, I want to encourage you to let someone who is grieving say the hard things. Let them be sad and not be okay without giving them instructions on how to process "correctly." Pro tip: there is no "right" way.

9. Pray for them and over them

I know this made the list for words to say, but prayer is an action—and a powerful one at that. Matthew 21:21–22 says, "So Jesus answered and said to them, 'Assuredly, I say to you, if you have faith and do not doubt, you will not only do what was done to the fig tree, but also if you say to this mountain, 'Be removed and be cast into the sea,' it will be done. And whatever things you ask in prayer, believing, you will receive.'" Pray for peace (Philippians 4:7), pray for comfort (Matthew 5:14), pray for provision (Philippians 4:19), pray for strength (2 Corinthians 12:9), and pray for His presence to be felt (Psalm 34:18).

Please friends, pray in your quiet places, pray when you are together, and pray over texts. Prayer can change everything.

10. Send a card!

I have kept every note and/or card from those who both attended the funeral and those who sent cards afterward. From time to time, I will pull them out because I need to feel loved on or to remind myself of who God has given to me to be in "my corner." I especially love the ones that share a wonderful memory of my brother or those that have Scriptures all throughout them. (I once sent a card with index cards full of Scriptures for a friend to put all over her house. It is a great way to surround them with hope in what feels like a hopeless situation.)

11. Offer childcare

If I can give a standing ovation to every person who has watched my children during this season, I would. Because when I am trying to take care of things that are especially hard and heavy, I don't always want my boys around to experience it with me. And when I am a heaping ball of a mess, it means the world to have a friend take my children to let them have fun and not have a front row seat to mom's grief. Not that they should be sheltered from the process of grief, I think it is important that we show our kids how to struggle with big things leaning into God for our every need, but because I don't want Michael or Jacob to get the blunt end of a sleep-deprived, emotion-filled, grieving woman who needs Jesus in that moment (and maybe coffee, food, and a nap), I phone a friend. I want to be a good mom, and sometimes being a good mom means taking a break.

12. Clean their house

This one could go either way for some who prefer personal space but as someone who is easily embarrassed by my house being a hot mess—someone doing my dishes, or dusting my blinds, or mopping my floors sounds like the greatest act of kindness. Even taking a dog for a walk is a beautiful thing. Like I said before, when you feel like you need an award for getting out of bed, there's a chance your house will be the last thing getting any attention, but it is also one of the first things that make us feel happy and safe.

13. Be a gatekeeper

This one I save for last but it is a very important role to have. When a family is making arrangements or you are trying to have some privacy with the story surrounding a loved ones passing or you are trying to prevent a continual slew of visitors from interrupting your family time while they drop off gift cards and other items, it is vital to have a gatekeeper. Someone outside the family who everything can funnel through. Who won't be emotional or loose-lipped but will respect the wishes of the family and love them by keeping boundaries in place. A gatekeeper is a bridge or a go between when a family is feeling especially vulnerable and is needing to feel protected. I love the gatekeepers.

If you feel up to the task, up to being strong when even the strongest feel weak, offer to do this.

Works Cited

Henry, Matthew. *Matthew Henry's Commentary on the Whole Bible.* Vol. VI Acwts to Revelation. 6 vols. London, England, 1706.

Kübler-Ross, Elisabeth. *Death: The Final Stage of Growth.* Upper Saddle River, New Jersey: Prentice Hall, Inc., 1975.

Merriam-Webster. *Dictionary "Hope".* n.d. https://www.merriam-webster.com/dictionary/hope (accessed June 2019, 2019).

Swindoll, Charles R. "What Is Sovereignty?" In *The Mystery of God's Will: What Does He Want from Me?* by Charles R. Swindoll. Nashville, Tennessee: Thomas Nelson, 2001.

TerKeurst, Lysa. *It's Not Supposed to Be This Way: Finding Unexpected Strength When Disappointments Leave You Shattered.* Nashville, Tennessee: Thomas Nelson, 2018.

Wickham, Phil. "Tears of Joy." *The Ascension.* Comps. Pete Kipley and Phil Wickham. 9. 2013. CD.

CPSIA information can be obtained
at www.ICGtesting.com
Printed in the USA
LVHW010122150920
666005LV00008B/23

9 781400 327461